THE MEN WHO CREATED GUNDAM

Translator: Jason Moses
Proofreading: Patrick Sutton
Cover Design: Glen Isip
Production: Glen Isip
Nicole Dochych
Brandon Bovia

First published in Japan in 2014 by KADOKAWA CORPORATION, Tokyo
English Translation rights arranged with KADOKAWA CORPORATION, Tokyo through TUTTLE-MORI AGENCY, INC., Tokyo
Published in English by DENPA, LLC., Portland, Oregon 2022

Originally published in Japanese as *"Gundam" wo Tsukutta Otokotachi*, parts 1 & 2 by KADOKAWA CORPORATION, 2014
The Men Who Created Gundam originally serialized as *Gundam Sousei* in Vols. 5-9 of *Kidou Senshi Gundam-san* by KADOKAWA, 2009-2011. *Tomino Legends* originally serialized as *TominoDen* in NewType Ace Iss. 1-7 by KADOKAWA, 2011-2012.

This is a work of fiction.

ISBN-13: 978-1-634429-74-0
Library of Congress Control Number: 2021943396
Printed in the USA

First Edition

Denpa, LLC.
625 NW 17th Ave
Portland, OR 97209
www.denpa.pub

Reproduced Pages

Pg. 116 ("Mechanical Design")
Mobile Suit Gundam Complete Works, vol. 2

Pg. 246–247 ("Wrap Party")
Mobile Suit Gundam Complete Works, vol. 5
Animec #8

Pg. 290 ("Confirming the *Gundam* Movie")
Nikkan Sports - October 2, 1980

Pg. 291 ("Announcing the *Gundam* Movie")
Gekkan OUT, December 1980
Animec #15

Pg. 340 ("*Mobile Suit Gundam Complete Works*")
Mobile Suit Gundam Complete Works, vol. 1
Animec #15

Pg. 466–468 ("The New Anime Century Declaration")
Yomiuri Shimbun, February 6, 1981
Yomiuri Shimbun, February 23, 1981

Thanks

Nikkan Sports News
Asahi Paper Co., Ltd.
Hironori Katayama
Bandai Co., Ltd.
The Yomiuri Shimbun
Shochiku Co., Ltd.

Special Thanks

Sunrise Koji Nakajima
Emi Hotoda
Ichiro Itano
Makoto Togashi
Masanobu Komaki

Yoshikazu Yasuhiko Kunio Okawara
Yoshiyuki Tomino

THE MEN WHO CREATED GUNDAM

The chapters contained in this volume were originally included under the name *Gundam Genesis* in volumes 5-9 of ***Mobile Suit Gundam-San*** (Kadokawa). The people and events depicted within are based on reality—with some embellishments.
Tomino Legends originally ran in *New Type Ace* vol. 1-7.

In 1978, an anime series was born
in a small corner of Tokyo.

With the help of countless allies,
it achieved nationwide recognition,
became a movie series, and changed the
history of Japanese animation forever.

Its name was *Mobile Suit Gundam*,
and this... is its story.

Contents

THE MEN WHO CREATED
GUNDAM

Note: *Natsuko's Summer* was a 1979 ad campaign for Japanese cosmetics company Shiseido. "Sexual Violet Number One" is a single released by rock singer/songwriter Masahiro Kuwana on July 21, 1979.

EPISODE 1

KLAM

A STUDIO SOMEWHERE IN TOKYO.

Sexual Violet No. 1

SHISEIDO

—1979.

Natsuko's Summer

KLAK

KLAK

KLAK

KLAK

AMURO RAY'S VOICE ACTOR
TORU FURUYA

YOU HIT ME AGAIN?!

EVEN MY FATHER NEVER HIT ME!

JOLT

CUT!

MRRMR

WHAT! YOU DEAF OR SOMETHING?

RMBLLL

EPISODE
1

FWOOM

GENERAL DIRECTOR YOSHIYUKI TOMINO

I SAID CUT, KID.

...
SIR.

MRRMR
IT'S BEEN TEN TAKES ALREADY.
AREN'T YOU BEING A LITTLE HARSH?
AT THE TIME, FURUYA'S ROLE AS HYUMA HOSHI IN *STAR OF THE GIANTS* STILL LOOMED LARGE.
EVERY PRO GOES THROUGH A TRIAL LIKE THIS...

KLAKA
FREEING HIMSELF FROM THIS PHANTOM OF HIS PAST TOOK CONSIDERABLE STRUGGLE.
OKAY, BACK TO WORK.
SCENE 17, TAKE 11!

I WON'T BACK DOWN! I'LL ENDURE THIS AS LONG AS IT TAKES!
OKAY!

HANG IN THERE, FURUYA!
FRAW BOW'S VOICE ACTRESS RUMIKO UKAI

YOU HIT ME AGAIN?! EVEN MY FATHER NEVER HIT ME!
RAWR

WELL?
HOW'D YA LIKE THAT?

OOOH!

なんちゅうか本中華

SHOOM
DIRECT-OR?

KRRK

SHMM
U-UM...

BWOOMPH

ガクッ

GWA UGH!

THUD

D- DIRECTOR!

DAMMIT... YOU REALLY HATE THE IDEA OF HYUMA HOSHI BEING AMURO THAT MUCH, HUH?

YOU SHOULD JUST DO IT YOURSELF, THEN!

THE LINE...

HUH?
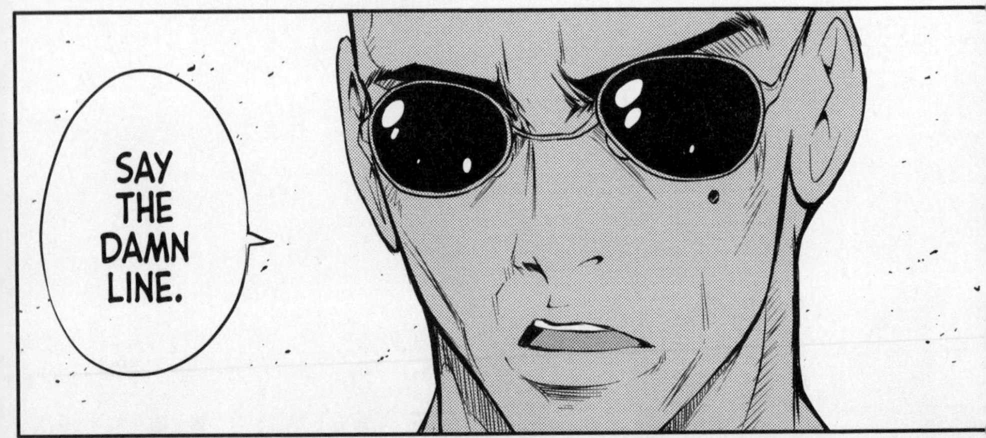
SAY THE DAMN LINE.

FWP

YA HIT ME.

RMBL
THAT WAS A TOTALLY DIFFERENT READ.
WH-WHAT'S HE GOING FOR?

KA-
BRACK

ズッ

VWSHHH
SQWK
PTOO
KLIK

You hit me again?! Even my father never hit me!
!
SHDDR
SHDD
HE'S LIKE A DIFFERENT PERSON NOW.
RMBLLL
WHAT A MONSTER.
SHWP
TOOK A WHILE.
AH, OWWIE
SHWP

I GUESS YOU CAN ACT WHEN YOU ACTUALLY GIVE A DAMN.

I KNEW IT... HE WAS JUST TRYING TO DRAW OUT MY POTENTIAL!

I'VE GOT THIS!

FURUYA, TAKING OFF!

SCENE 17!

TAKE 12!

WE'RE ROLLING!

カラ
KLAK
カラ
KLAK
ACTION!
AND THAT'S WHY WE'RE STILL TALKING ABOUT THIS SCENE DECADES LATER.

NOT THAT ANYONE KNEW AT THE TIME.

NO ONE HAD ANY IDEA THIS SHOW WOULD BECOME A LEGEND THAT ROCKED JAPAN—AND THE WORLD.

MORNING.
PAT
さわ
EEP!
HANDS OFF, BUSTER!
PKOW
ハム
OUCH!
YOW...
WELL, EXCEPT FOR THIS GUY.
WHAT? YOUR ASS UNDER LOCK AND KEY OR SOMETHING?

Note: The Candies were a Japanese idol trio active from 1973-1978.

ドオーン
BWAAAM
YOSHIKAZU YASUHIKO! A GENIUS WHOSE GORGEOUS LINEWORK KNOWS NO LIMITS!
EPISODE 2

A FINE MORNING TO YOU, MASTER YASUHIKO.

MORNING.

ムシャ

SNARF

ムシャ

SNARF

HE AND I GO BACK A WAYS.

WUH? THAT FILTHY LAY-ABOUT?

F-FORGIVE ME!

JOLT

RMBLLL

MUNCH

PROJECT PROPOSAL
"FREEDOM FIGHTER
GUNBOY" (TBD)
BAPF

...
WHAT IS THIS?
WHAT IT LOOKS LIKE. PROPOSAL FOR A NEW SHOW.
I, UH,
RRMMM
WANT YOU ON BOARD FOR IT.

HEH. I SHOULD HAVE KNOWN. ANOTHER TOY COMMERCIAL.
SORRY.
I DON'T DO THAT KIND OF WORK ANYMORE.
'SCUSE ME?
SPACE BATTLESHIP YAMATO... ARRIVEDERCI YAMATO... OFFICE ACADEMY IS IN THE BUSINESS OF MAKING MEGA HITS.
WE MAKE MOVIE HISTORY.
WHAT YOU SEE HERE ARE THE FRUITS OF THAT LABOR.
THIS OFFICE...
OUR BOUNTIFUL PRODUCTION BUDGETS...
YOU UNDERSTAND, DON'T YOU? YOU AND I...
WE LIVE IN DIFFERENT WORLDS.
YEAH.
I GUESS SO.
SORRY TO BOTHER YOU. I'M LEAVING THE PROPOSAL, FEEL FREE TO LOOK IT OVER WHEN YOU HAVE TIME.
I WILL.
SLAM
バタン

HRM.

カラ
CLNK

IT'S JUST NOT FLOWING TODAY. I SUPPOSE I SHOULD CALL IT A DAY.

GET ME A TABLE AT MAXIM'S DE PARIS IN GINZA.

RIGHT AWAY, SIR.

DIDN'T I ASK YOU TO THROW THAT AWAY?

AH! T-TERRIBLY SORRY! I'LL DO IT NOW!

FLP
YOU CAN'T WORK ON TRASH LIKE THIS FOREVER, TOMI–
PROJECT PROPOSAL
"FREEDOM FIGHTER
GUNBOY" (TBD)
GRP
GRTT
YOSHIYUKI TOMINO, YOU BASTARD!
TRMBL
TRMBL

VRRROOM
VWWOOOM
KCHNK

NIPPON SUNRISE
KREEK
KREEK
HAKK!! KOFF!!
THIS PLACE ALWAYS WAS FILTHY!
BAM
TOMINO!
ARE YOU HERE, TOMINO?!
KRRK
YO.

WHAT IS THE MEANING OF THIS?!
SHWF
NOT MUCH. JUST A RUN-OF-THE-MILL ROBOT CARTOON.
SHIT, THAT'S COLD!
A GLORIFIED 30-MINUTE COMMERCIAL.
BAM

THIS IS A SERIOUS SCI-FI DRAMA!
PROJECT PROPOSAL
"FREEDOM FIGHTER GUNBOY" (TBD)
I DON'T KNOW HOW YOU MANAGED TO FOOL THE SPONSORS,
BUT THIS IS UNLIKE ANY ROBOT ANIME THAT'S BEEN MADE BEFORE!
IT'S TOO SOON FOR WHAT YOU'RE ATTEMPTING.
A DECADE AHEAD OF THE TIMES AT LEAST!
THE VIEWERS WON'T BE ABLE TO KEEP UP!
GRRAAW
ムわっ
コトッ
KLOK
SLIME
THEN WE'LL DRAG THEM,
KICKING AND SCREAMING,
TEN YEARS INTO THE FUTURE.

SHNG
WE WILL, WILL WE?
WE'RE NOT THE ONES WHO DECIDE WHEN.
ROOOOAR
THE AUDIENCE DOES!
I'VE MADE ALL KINDS OF ANIME.
BUT RIGHT NOW, RIGHT HERE, THIS IS THE ONE I'M BURNING TO MAKE.
PROJECT PROPOSA
"FREEDOM FI
GUNBOY"
AND IF SOMEONE'S BURNING TO MAKE THIS THING...
SHKK

THEN YOU KNOW WHAT...

SOMEONE'S GONNA WANT TO WATCH IT, TOO.

SPARE ME YOUR SELF-SERVING LOGIC.

THEN WHY'D YOU DRAG YOUR ASS OUT HERE?
BIG FAN OF RUNDOWN SHACKS IN KAMI-IGUSA?

I JUST...
THE PROPOSAL'S T.B.D.
BUT I'VE ALREADY DECIDED ON THE FINAL TITLE.
フゥー
PHFFF
THE TITLE?
ゴゴゴゴ
RMBLLL

MOBILE SUIT GUNDAM.

GUN... DAM?
AND SO, IN A TINY CORNER OF TOKYO,
GUNDAM LET OUT ITS FIRST, TINY CRY.

IN TIME, IT WOULD BECOME A GIANT, TOWERING OVER EVEN *YAMATO*.

BUT FOR NOW, IT YET SLUMBERED IN THE CRIB.

EPISODE
3
SUNSHINE 60
NOW OPEN
AUTUMN, 1978
TODAY, AN AUDITION WILL TAKE PLACE THAT WILL SEND SHOCKWAVES THROUGH ANIME HISTORY.
MOBILE SUIT GUNDAM
Auditions for the role of AMURO RAY
AMURO, TAKING OFF!
AMURO, TAKING OFF!
HEY, BOYO!
HRK!
TORU FURUYA
AGE: 25

EPISODE
3
One Cup

LEMME A HAND, WILLYA?
MY LEGS AIN'T WORKIN'.

S-SURE...
WOAH, WHO'S THIS BOOZE-HOUND?

OOF, HE STINKS OF ALCOHOL!
BWEHHH

SO, WHERE SHOULD I TAKE YOU?

I NEED TO DITCH HIM AND GET TO THE AUDITION.

HUH?

THERE. OVER THERE.

MOBILE SUIT GUNDAM

Auditions for the role of AMURO RAY

YOU'RE JOKING.

YOU'RE AUDITIONING FOR THE AMURO ROLE TOO?

SURE AM. SHUICHI IKEDA.

HIC

PLEASURE.

...

AMURO, TAKING OFF!

THAT'S THE TICKET!

HE'S A GOOD FIT, EH, CHIEF?

I'VE HEARD WORSE.

OKAY! GREAT WORK IN THERE, FURUYA!
WHO'S UP NEXT?

MUCH APPRECIATED!
WELL, I DID MY BEST! JUST GOTTA WAIT FOR THE RESULTS.
KCHAK

IKEDA? WHAT ARE YOU DOING OUT HERE?
HUH?
AW, SCREW YOU, PAL!
I'M SOBER AS A JUDGE!
YEAH, AND YOU'RE ABOUT TO GET TRIED FOR CONTEMPT OF COURT!
BOP
JUST GET IN THERE!
HERE COMES SHUICHI IKEDA!
HOOO-EEEY
WHO'S THIS DRUNK?
WHAT'S THE WORD, DIRECTOR?
FWAAH
GIVE HIM A SHOT.
MAYBE WE CAN USE HIM FOR SOME-THING.

OKAY, WHENEVER YOU'RE READY, IKEDA!
SHURE! UM...
ARROW... AMOO... MORROW?
EYY!
AROMU, BLASTIN' RIGHT ON OFF!
THE NAME'S AMURO! A-MU-RO! READ THE SCRIPT!
I'M READING THE SHIT OUT OF IT, THOUGH!
YOU SEEN THE LETTERS? THEY'RE TINY!
ぼやー
WOOGH
AMURO TAKING...
TAKING... UH...
SHIT.
URPH!

BWAAARF
HRK!
WHOA ...

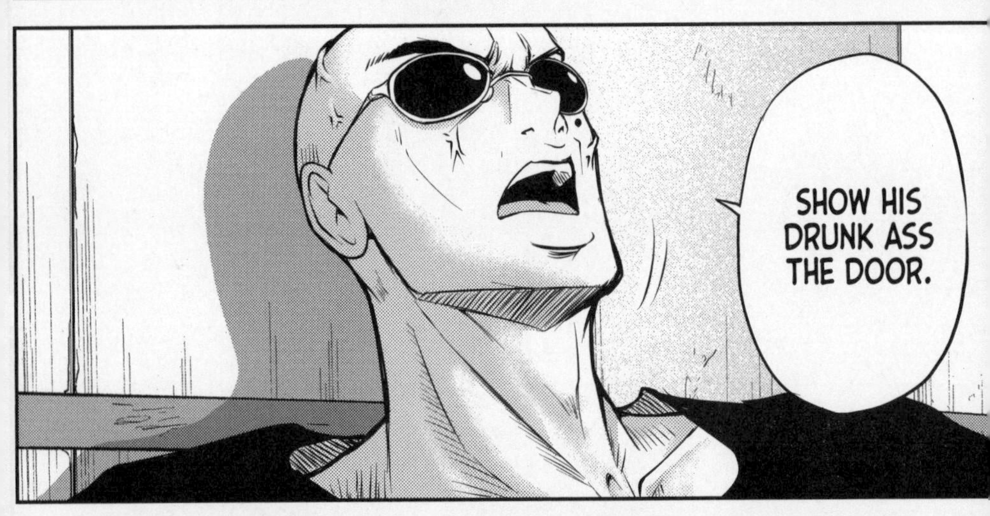

SO WHAT WAS THAT AUDITION FOR ANYWAY?
THE HELL DID YOU EVEN SHOW UP HERE FOR?
THIS!
MOBILE SUIT GUNDAM!
機動戦士
ガンダム
GUNDAM
OH, SHIT. ROBOTS.
AIN'T THAT SOMETHI-
RRRRIP
WHAT ARE YOU-
KRNCH

CHAR AZNABLE
ゴゴゴ
RMMMBL
ゴゴ

KRRK
DIRECTOR!
IKEDA?
WHAT'S GOING ON?
SHWF

I DON'T SUPPOSE
YOU'D LET ME AUDITION FOR *THIS* GUY?

GIVE ME A BREAK! YOU COULDN'T EVEN GET AMURO'S NAME RIGHT!
Y-YEAH! GO HOME!

FUCKIN' LOUD-MOUTHS!
AN ACTOR WHO FORGETS THE ROLE HE'S PLAYING AFTER A LITTLE ALCOHOL IS NO ACTOR AT ALL.

JUST LET ME DO IT. I WON'T WASTE YOUR TIME.

HOW'D THIS SONUVABITCH SOBER UP SO FAST?!

ALL RIGHT, THEN.
LET'S HEAR IT.

KLAK カラ KLAKA カラ

OKAY, STARTING THE TEST!

YOUR LINE IS–

DON'T WORRY.

CHAR'S INSIDE ME. ***HE'LL*** KNOW WHAT TO SAY.

HUH?

ゴゴ
ゴゴゴゴ
RRRMBLLLL

One does not care to acknowledge the mistakes of one's youth.

!

ゴシ
SWP
ゴシ
SWP

AM I CRAZY, OR WAS CHAR IN THE BOOTH JUST NOW?!

WELL?

D-DIRECTOR!

HEH!
ACTORS ARE CURIOUS CREATURES, AREN'T THEY?

A DISGUSTING DRUNK ONE MINUTE, AND A LEGEND OF THE UNIVERSAL CENTURY THE NEXT.
BLOWS MY MIND.
MAKE NO MISTAKE. THE GUY IN THERE RIGHT NOW
IS CHAR AZNABLE HIMSELF.
THE LUCKIEST ACTORS ARE THOSE WHO FIND A ROLE THAT ONLY THEY CAN PLAY.
SHUICHI IKEDA HAD FOUND HIS.
THIS ENCOUNTER WOULD ONLY ACCELERATE *GUNDAM*'S FUSION REACTION IN THE MONTHS TO COME.
BUT THAT'S A STORY FOR ANOTHER TIME.

THE MEN WHO CREATED
GUNDAM

Project Proposals for *Space Combat Team Gunboy* and *Mobile Steelman Gunboy*.

▼▶ The project proposals have simple designs printed on blue paper, and were included as a bonus with the recent Blu-Ray release of *Mobile Suit Gundam* TV.

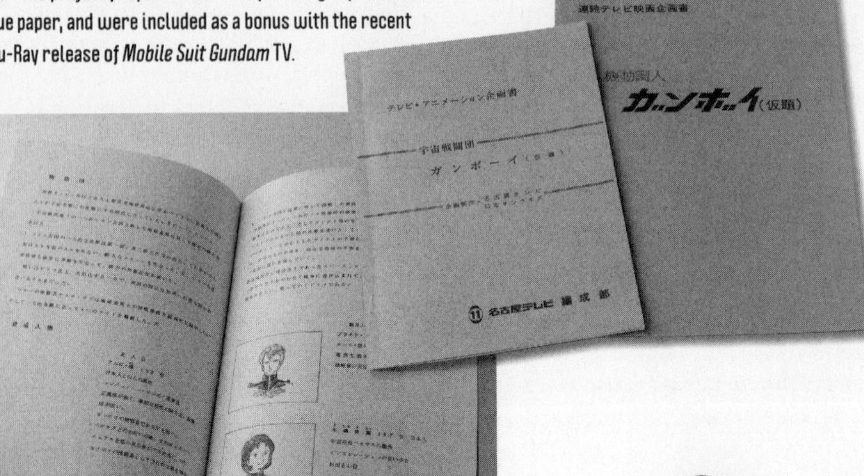

An early design for the Gundam.

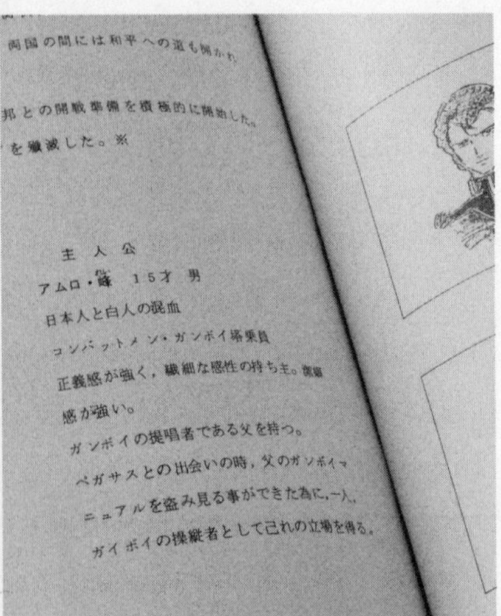
両国の間には和平への道も開かれ

邦との開戦準備を積極的に開始した。

を殲滅した。※

主人公

アムロ・嶺 15才 男

日本人と白人の混血

コンバットメン・ガンボイ搭乗員

正義感が強く，繊細な感性の持ち主。使命感が強い。

ガンボイの提唱者である父を持つ。

ペガサスとの出会いの時，父のガンボイマニュアルを盗み見る事ができた為に，一人，ガンボイの操縦者として己れの立場を得る。

▲▶ An early Gundam design, and a page from a later project proposal. Amuro's profile is nearly unchanged from the final draft.

Courtesy of: Sunrise

Project Proposals: *Freedom Fighter Gunboy* (TBD)

In the story you just read, Yoshiyuki Tomino presents Yoshikazu Yasuhiko with a project proposal for a show called *Freedom Fighter Gunboy*. This was, in fact, the actual name Tomino chose during the initial planning stages. When the show appeared before us on April 7, 1979, it did so as *Mobile Suit Gundam*.

The plan was originally intended as a follow-up to Tomino's previous super robot shows: 1977's *Super Machine Zambot 3*, and 1978's *The Unchallengeable Daitarn 3*. Tomino's penchant for complex plotting ensured neither show was a simple good-versus-evil affair, and *Gunboy*'s project proposal would take this even further. A clear-cut ensemble drama set amidst warring factions. Robots portrayed as weapons to more seamlessly weave them into the fabric of the story. Characters driven by principles and ideologies on both sides of the conflict. All of these elements were present from the very outset.

The proposal for *Space Combat Team Gunboy*, created for Nippon Sunrise (currently Sunrise Inc.) and the Nagoya Broadcasting Network, featured a battle between Earthlings and Aliens—standard fare for robot anime at the time. The enemy faction was the Zeon *Empire*, and the battle raged across a different star system from our own. And with a mostly Japanese cast, the show lacked the multicultural feel of the *Gundam* we know.

As revisions continued, the show now known as *Mobile Steelman Gunboy* switched to using the Anno Domini calendar. Space colonies entered the picture, the Empire became a Principality, and now-familiar organizations like the Earth Federation appeared at last. Though some names remained different from their finalized versions, the story was now a grittier one, pitting humans against each other in the quagmire of war.

Though these project proposals and their revisions reveal the unmistakable skeleton of *Gundam*, we also catch a glimpse of the cunning we witness from Yoshiyuki Tomino in this very manga. The production team and sponsors had strict demands. Tomino had to meet them while still reaching the core robot anime audience and including a gritty ensemble drama that was, in the words of Yasuhiko, "A decade ahead of its time." He accomplished this by taking the robot anime format established in *Daitarn 3* and slowly working the DNA to form something new. To accomplish this while satisfying both the audience and the sponsors was to attempt a truly titanic feat, indeed. ◆

THE MEN WHO CREATED
GUNDAM

NIPPON SUNRISE
Note: *Watashi no Don* is Mako Ishino's 1978 second single.
EPISODE 4
ZZZZ
ZZZZ
Watashi no D
Mako Ishi
DIRECTOR, DIRECTOR!
MR. TOMINO!
DASH
BAM
THEY'RE HERE, THEY'RE HERE!
HAAH
HAAH
BWUH?
NIPPON SUNRISE PRODUCTION ASSISTANT MOMOE KUSAKARI

Bwaaah
GEEZ, YOU'RE LOUD. WHO'S HERE? MAKO ISHINO?
PLEASE TELL ME YOU WEREN'T EXPECTING AN IDOL!
ガムャ
KCHNK
GUNDAM'S SPONSOR IS HERE!
ドオオオオン
BWOOOM
ゴゴゴゴゴ
RRMMBLL
TOY COMPANY PRESIDENT
SHICHIRO KUROBA
THAT OLD FOGEY? PAIN IN MY ASS...
ボリボリ
POP

EPISODE
4
IT'S GONNA BE A LONG DAY.

I SAW THE DESIGNS FOR THE WHITE BASE AND GUNDAM.
NOT BAD! CONSIDER ME A FAN.
THANKS.
THERE'S JUST ONE THING I DON'T LOVE.
IS THERE NOW?
FWAP
IS A PURE WHITE ROBOT REALLY CUT OUT FOR A STARRING ROLE?
HOW ABOUT ADDING A LITTLE COLOR?
WITH ALL DUE RESPECT, SIR.
THERE ARE NO COLORFUL WEAPONS IN THIS WORLD.

FROM FIGHTER JETS TO NUCLEAR-POWERED AIRCRAFT CARRIERS...
MODERN WEAPONS HAVE SIMPLE COLOR SCHEMES.
GUNDAM IS A BATTLEFIELD DRAMA.
A WHITE ROBOT IS THE ONLY CHOICE IF WE WANT TO CONVEY A REALISTIC STORY.
SHF
SHKK
SZZ
PWAAH
I'M SORRY, BUT WHAT DO YOU THINK WE'RE DOING HERE?

WHAT DO I THINK I'M–
WHO ASKED YOU TO DESIGN *WEAPONS?*
I TOLD YOU TO MAKE A SHOW TO SELL TOYS TO CHILDREN!
YOU DON'T GET IT.
YOU WANT TO TELL A WAR DRAMA?
GRR
YOUR ANIME AIN'T WORTH SHIT IF IT ISN'T SELLING SOMETHING!
BAM
わなわな
TRMBL
YOU'RE THE ONE WHO DOESN'T GET IT.

WITH KIDS THESE DAYS, YOU NEED TO BLOW THEIR FRIGGIN' MINDS!
OTHERWISE, THEY WON'T EVEN LOOK AT THE DAMN SCREEN!
GAWR
THAT'S YOUR WHOLE JOB DESCRIP-TION!
SAY THAT AGAIN, ASSHOLE!
THE DIRECTOR'S DYING ON THAT HILL, HUH...
...
BAM
SHWIP
EXCUSE ME!
カキ カキ
SKRT
BOOM
IS THIS TO YOUR LIKING, SIR?

OOH! WHITE, WITH RED, BLUE, AND YELLOW ACCENTS! THE KIDS DO SO LOVE THEIR PRIMARY COLORS!

NOW THIS IS SOMETHING I CAN SELL! *GWAHAHA!*

BAAAM

STAND DOWN, TOMINO.

YOU WANT TO CREATE SOMETHING A DECADE AHEAD OF ITS TIME?

ゴゴゴゴ
RRMMMBBLL

BOTH TOMINO AND YOSHIKAZU HAD ONCE WORKED AT ANIME STUDIO MUSHI PRODUCTIONS. THERE THE SHOW WAS KING. BUT A WANTON DISREGARD FOR PROFITS EVENTUALLY LED THE COMPANY TO BANKRUPTCY.

THIS WAS A CONVERSATION THAT COULD ONLY OCCUR BETWEEN THOSE WHO HAD SEEN SUCH STRUGGLE FIRSTHAND.

HMPH. FINE.

OH, YEAH. ABOUT THE ENEMY ROBOT DESIGNS...

HM?

WHAT OF IT? KIDS WON'T BUY A ROBOT THAT ONLY EXISTS TO GET TURNED TO SCRAP.

DO WHATEVER YOU WANT.

HMPH!
YOU BET YOUR ASS I WILL.

VRRMMM

VRRRMM
HEH. LOOK AT ME, SHOUTING AT MY AGE.
I'M NOT SURE THAT'S GOOD FOR YOU, SIR.

YOSHIYUKI TOMINO... CURIOUS FELLOW.
BUT REALLY, WE NEED TO LEAVE MEN LIKE HIM TO THEIR OWN DEVICES.
NIPPON SUNRISE
VRRRRM

"DO WHAT YOU WANT! I'LL TAKE FULL RESPONSIBILITY."

IN A PERFECT WORLD,

THAT'S WHAT I WOULD HAVE SAID.

BUT REALITY BEGS TO DIFFER.

WE CAN'T OFFER SPONSORSHIPS IF WE DON'T SELL TOYS.

AND TO SELL, WE NEED TO MAKE DEMANDS.

KLNK

KLNK

THESE ARE COLD AND INDIFFERENT TIMES WE'RE LIVING IN, DON'T YOU THINK?

SIR...

THEY'LL UNDERSTAND, IN DUE TIME.
ブロロロ
VRROOM
HEH. IF ONLY.

YOU'LL PAY FOR THIS, SHITHEAD!
COULD YOU PLEASE WAIT UNTIL THEY'RE OUT OF EARSHOT?

HMPH. LET'S GO, THEN.
NIPPON SUNRIS
HUH? GO WHERE?
THE MASTER'S WORKSHOP.

GRRRN
GRRRN
OKAWARA DESIGNS
SPECIALIZING IN MECHANICAL DESIGNS
☎(12)3456
WHRRR
KLANG
KLANG

OKAWARA DESIGNS
SPECIALIZING IN MECHANICAL DESIGNS
☎(12)3456
VREE
KLANG

HEY, POPS! YOU IN THERE?

WREE

YOU WANT ME TO DAMAGE MY BLADE?

MECHA DESIGNER
KUNIO OKAWARA

KCH

WHAT'S THIS?

I'VE GOT A DESIGN REQUEST FOR YOU.

AN ENEMY MECHA.

Gunboy Enemy Design
Air Intake Duct
Monoeye
Empty Space
Ducts
Radar
Front view camera window
Rear Camera Eye
Radar Port
Gun
Maintenance Entrance
Moves front to back
Moves Horizontally
Radar
Rear Gun
Frontal Armor
Joint cover
Rocket Nozzles
Rear Camera
When compared to a human
Making the shoulder more narrow will make it less mobile
Maybe extend this way?
Manual Rescue Port
This doesn't look possible

I WONDER WHAT KIND OF REQUEST IT IS...

WHAT THE?

IT LOOKS SO OUTDATED. ISN'T THIS SHOW SUPPOSED TO BE AHEAD OF ITS TIME?

HRM...

THIS'LL TAKE A WHILE.

GIMME THREE DAYS.

YOU GOT IT.

JUST ONE THING, DIRECTOR.

OKAWARA DESIGNS

DO I REALLY HAVE THE GO-AHEAD TO FOLLOW THIS SPEC?

HUH? WHAT IS HE ASKING FOR?
YEAH, OF COURSE. I JUST TALKED TO THE SPONSOR'S GEEZER.
HE GAVE ME CARTE BLANCHE TO DO WHAT I WANT.

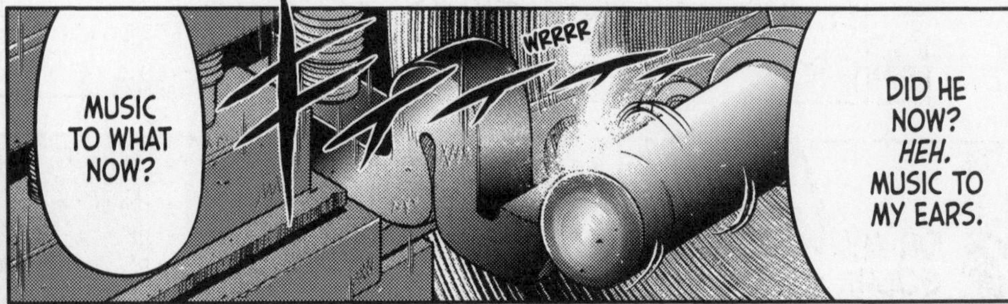

DID HE NOW? *HEH.* MUSIC TO MY EARS.
WRRRR
MUSIC TO WHAT NOW?

HAHAHA. PLAYING COY, HUH? YOU'RE ONE SLY FOX.

HEH.

BWAHA HAHA! AH HA HA HA!

HAHAHA HAHA!

Ha Ha Ha Ha Ha

?

THREE DAYS LATER.

NIPPON SUNRISE

THE PACKAGE FROM OKAWARA ARRIVED!

HUH. AWFULLY BIG BOX FOR SOME DESIGN SHEETS.
FWPH
OH MY GOSH!

THIS
IS THE
BAD GUY
ROBOT?

PROTOTYPE
WOW, IT'S GOT EVERYTHING FROM DESIGN SHEETS TO A WOODEN MODEL.
MOST IMPOR-TANTLY...
IT'S COOL!
IF YOU TOLD ME IT CAME FROM THAT PROPOSAL, I'D CALL YOU CRAZY!
IF YOU HAVEN'T FIGURED IT OUT, THAT SHEET LIKELY EXPLAINED HOW THE ROBOT'S USED.
THEY'VE WORKED OUT A CONSENSUS OF SORTS, SO THAT'S ALL THEY NEED.
DOES THAT MEAN-

TOMINO MIGHT AS WELL HAVE LEFT THE SHEET BLANK, AS FAR AS DESIGN DETAILS ARE CONCERNED.
HE LEFT IT ALL IN THE HANDS OF THE DESIGNER, KUNIO OKAWARA.
THE SPONSOR DOESN'T REALIZE IT, BUT THIS THING IS GOING TO BE THE SHOW'S HIDDEN HERO.

A HIDDEN HERO? OH... I GET IT NOW!
HE SNUCK THE DESIGN PAST THE SPONSOR...

AND HE USED THE WHITE BASE AND GUNDAMS AS DECOYS!
THE ZAKU WASN'T A ONE-OFF ENEMY. IT APPEARED THROUGHOUT THE SHOW.

IN FACT, THE NEXT ENEMY MS—THE GOUF—DOESN'T APPEAR UNTIL EPISODE 12, TO CAP OFF THE FIRST COUR.

ZAKUS EVEN APPEAR IN THE LAST EPISODE.

IT'S BEEN OVER 30 YEARS SINCE THE ORIGINAL BROADCAST,

BUT THE ZAKU IS STILL SHARING THE SPOTLIGHT WITH THE GUNDAM TO THIS VERY DAY.

Note: *Yosaku Chops Wood* by Kiminori Nanasawa.

RRRAAAAHHH
HAS BECOME A BATTLEFIELD!
AAAGHH! I BLEW IT!
OKAY, WHO TOOK MY PEGBAR?!
EPISODE
5

RARR
RARR
DAMMIT, WHY DOES THE WHITE BASE HAVE SO MANY FREAKIN' LINES IN IT?!

WHO DESIGNED THIS THING?!

PAT
OKAWARA DESIGNS
I DID. SORRY ABOUT THAT, KIDDO.

N-NO WORRIES! THE DESIGN'S COPACETIC, MR. OKAWARA!
THANKS.
THE DESIGN FOR THE MUSAI'S FINISHED.
GREAT. GO AHEAD AND LEAVE IT HERE.

RAAR

HECK OF A RUCKUS IN HERE.

GUNDAM'S A DESIGN-HEAVY SHOW.

PLUS, THE END OF *DAITARN 3* OVERLAPS WITH NAGAHAMA'S *DALTANIOUS*. SO YEAH, IT'S HELL.

RAAR

RAAR

KANADA'S KEY FRAMES ARE READY!

SO ARE THE COLOR PROOFS FOR THE POSTERS!

BAM

BOOOSH

EEEK!

KSHA

WE'RE TOO BUSY FOR THIS GARBAGE!

YOWCH... IS YOUR ASS PROTECTED BY THE–

HM?

IT'S WHITE OUT HERE, TOO.
GOOONG
GOOONG
HAPPY NEW YEAR, EVERYONE!
GOOONG
A YEAR ENDS, ANOTHER BEGINS
0:00

THE SUN ROSE ON 1979.

AND THE CREW FURIOUSLY WORKED THROUGH THEIR SCHEDULE.

BEFORE LONG, WINTER TURNED TO SPRING.

AND THEN...

APRIL 7TH WAS HERE.

THE DESTINED MOMENT.

NIPPON SUNRISE

TIK カチッ

TIK カチッ

TIK カチッ

TIK カチッ

TIK カチッ

UHF
ON OFF
ドヒュオオオ
BKSHOOOOM
MOEAGARE! MOEAGARE!
IT'S STARTED!
SHH!
EARTH'S BURGEONING POPULATIONS...
MY FIRST ANIME...
LOOK AT THAT... IT'S ON!
COMMANDER CHAR BUILT HIS CAREER ON THE BATTLEFIELD!
ONE DOES NOT CARE TO ACKNOWLEDGE THE MISTAKES OF ONE'S YOUTH.

DESTROY GUNDAM!

NEXT EPISODE: "DESTROY GUNDAM! WILL YOU BE ABLE TO SURVIVE?"

PLP

PLP

YEAH

NYA

CONGRATS, GENTLEMEN!
BAM
YOU'RE ALL VERY LUCKY.

AFTER ALL, YOU WERE THERE WHEN ANIMATION HISTORY CHANGED FOREVER.

GUNDAM RISING!

AFTER SEEING THE PROTAGONIST BOARD THE GUNDAM IN THIS FIRST EPISODE, WHO COULD WAIT TO SEE WHAT HAPPENS NEXT?

TRULY, IT WAS A DECLARATION OF A NEW CENTURY IN ROBOT ANIME!

GUNDAM WAS RISING— LITERALLY!

WRRRR

DASHHH
OR SO IT APPEARED…

BAM
THE RATINGS ARE IN!
THINK WE HIT 20%?
HAHA, SERIOUSLY? OUR LAST SHOW, DAITARN, DID DO PRETTY WELL.
15% SEEMS ABOUT RIGHT.
LET'S SEE, SATURDAY AT 5:30…
URK!

...ports	9.2%
Run! Pink Lady	10.8%
Mobile Suit Gundam	3.0%
Battle Fever J	12.9%

BDOOOOOM

3.0%

RRMMMMBL

TH-THREE PERCENT?

THAT'S IT?

Note: *Gundam*'s sponsor Clover, which is pronounced *kuro-ba* in phonetic Japanese.

THERE'S OUR ANSWER. SOONER THAN ANTICIPATED, TOO.

THE SHOW WAS A FAILURE!
A MISERABLE, ROTTEN, FAILURE!
THERE WERE REASONS ONE COULD POINT TO— A SATURDAY EVENING TIME SLOT, FOR EXAMPLE.
BUT *MOBILE SUIT GUNDAM*'S MAIDEN VOYAGE WAS PROVING TO BE A ROCKY ONE INDEED!
ALL HOPE WAS NOT LOST, HOWEVER!
HONK
HONK
SHINJUKU NI-CHOME, TOKYO.
アニメック
Animec
EDITORIAL
CHIEF! HEY, CHIEF!

WHAT IS IT? WHY ALL THE YELLING?
I'LL HAVE YOU KNOW I'M *VERY* BUSY!
HUFF
I'M DOING CHECKS ON *ANNE OF GREEN GABLES* RIGHT NOW!
HUFF
ANNE! OF *GREEN GABLES!*
EDITOR-IN-CHIEF OF ANIMEC
MASANOBU KOMAKI
YOU SHOULD REALLY CHECK OUT SOME OTHER SHOWS, TOO. HERE'S LAST WEEK'S.
YOU LOVE TO ANNOY ME, DON'T YOU?
WHAT'S THIS? *GUNDAM*? THIS IS A SHOW?
GUNDAM #1
THE NEW SUNRISE SHOW, CHIEF.
OH, SO IT'S A ROBOT ANIME?

I SUPPOSE I'LL JUST HAVE TO TAKE A LOOKSEE...
KCHNK
Betamax
SONY SL-8100

MOEAGARE! ♪
YOU KNOW, THOUGH, THAT DIANA FROM *ANNE OF GREEN GABLES*? TOTAL CUTIE!
SURE. JUST WATCH THE SHOW, OKAY?

THE KEY ANIMATION THIS WEEK IN PARTICULAR WAS REALLY–
HM?

WHAT IN ANIME'S NAME?

KCHNK

HUH?

YOU'RE STILL HERE, CHIEF?

SOMETHING WRONG? WHY ARE THE LIGHTS OUT?

SHMM

CALL IN THE TEAM FOR AN EMERGENCY MEETING!

WUH?

GET RID OF WHATEVER WE'RE OPENING THE NEXT ISSUE WITH! WE'RE DOING A *GUNDAM* SPECIAL FEATURE!
HOOEEE!
BDMP
BDMP
CHIEF?
GUNDAM MAY HAVE ONLY REACHED 3% OF THE VIEWING AUDIENCE...
BDMP
BDMP
BDMP
BUT THEY WERE THE EXACT PEOPLE IT NEEDED TO REACH.
SOMETHING GREAT AND UNKNOWABLE WAS STIRRING. WHEN IT AWOKE, IT WOULD BE TIME TO CELEBRATE.

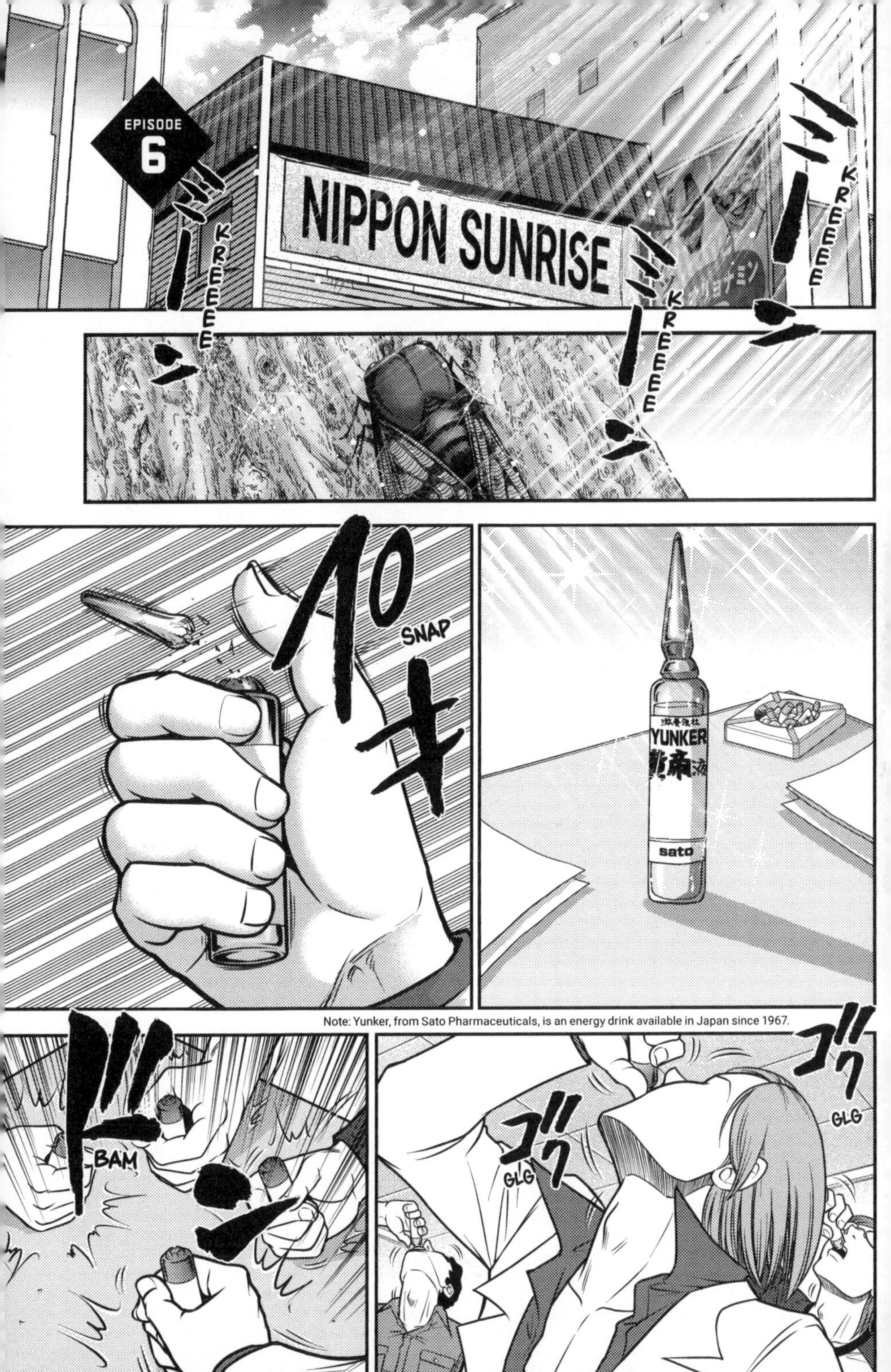

Note: Yunker, from Sato Pharmaceuticals, is an energy drink available in Japan since 1967.

OKAY, RAMBA RAL'S FINAL CUT IS FINISHED!
NEXT UP IS RYU JOSE'S! LET'S GO!
YEAAAH!
EPISODE 6

THIS IS REALLY REMINDING ME HOW AMAZING THIS SERIES IS.
RIGHT? IT'S TOTALLY DIFFERENT FROM EVERY ANIME I'VE EVER SEEN!
GRRP
WE REALLY ARE CREATING A NEW ERA OF ANIME!

BACK TO WORK, EVERYONE.
RIGHT!
NO GOOD?
NO GOOD.

WE HAVE LAST WEEK'S RATINGS FOR EPISODE 7, "THE CORE FIGHTER'S ESCAPE".
VIDEO RESEARCH PEGGED US AT 1.9%.
NIELSEN SAID THEY COULDN'T MEASURE US.
SO BASIC-ALLY—

WE HAD A RATING OF 0%?
THIS IS INSANE.
I EXPECTED A STRUGGLE, BUT THIS?

0% VIEWERSHIP!
A TRULY TERRIFYING STATISTIC FOR ANYONE WORKING IN TV!
YOUR SHOW MAY AS WELL BE CONDEMNED TO BROADCAST TO AN EMPTY VOID!

AT THIS RATE, WE'RE SCREWED.
WE NEED LEVERAGE.
SPECIFICALLY?

STARTING FROM THE STORY'S MIDPOINT, WE'LL HAVE NEW MECHA EVERY EPISODE.
NEW CANNON FODDER, SPECIFICALLY.
I'VE ALREADY COMMISSIONED THE DESIGNS FROM OKAWARA.

CANNON FODDER FOR THE GUNDAM TO DESTROY? *HA HA HA!* COME ON.
YOU'RE NOT PLANNING A RETURN TO A MONSTER-OF-THE-WEEK THING, ARE YOU?
WE'RE GIVING THE GUNDAM A POWER BOOST, TOO.
TAKE A GANDER AT THIS.

A POWER BOOST?
FLP
URK... M-MY WORD!

KABAM
G-ARMOR

RMMBLLL
ゴゴゴ
YOU'RE SERIOUS...

THE INSIDE OF THIS THING CAN HOUSE THE GUNDAM.
AFTER THE GUNDAM UNDOCKS, IT CAN COMBINE TO TURN INTO A FIGHTER JET.

IT *HOUSES* THE GUNDAM?
SO IF THE GUNDAM UNDOCKS FROM IT, THEN–
YOUR INTUITION'S SPOT ON. THE INSIDE'S HOLLOW.
COMPLETELY EMPTY.
COME ON, TOMINO.
THAT'S NOT A WEAPON. IT'S JUST A BOX.
INTRODUCE THIS THING, AND YOU'D OBLITERATE THE REALITY OF THE SHOW!
WHAT ARE YOU THINKING?

IT'D BE A PRETTY GROOVY TOY, RIGHT?
COOLEST BOX ON THE SHELF.

I ASKED YOU WHAT THE *HELL* YOU'RE THINKING, YOSHIYUKI TOMINO!
GRRNK
HE'S CRYING?
PLEASE. JUST GRIN AND BEAR IT, YASUHIKO.
PLP
I HAD NO OTHER CHOICE.
PLP

OUR SPONSOR SAID IF WE CAN JUST GET THE TOYS TO SELL, THEY'LL GIVE US A PASS ON THE RATINGS.
SO PLEASE!
TOMINO KNEW THAT A SUDDEN INFLUX OF ENEMY ROBOTS WOULD BE EXCRUCIATINGLY PAINFUL FOR HIS STAFF.
BUT SO BE IT.
IT WAS A PLEA STRAIGHT FROM HIS SOUL TO SEE *GUNDAM* COMPLETED.
PWF
ALL KINDS OF NEW WEAPONS MADE THEIR DEBUTS DURING WWII.
I'LL TELL THE CREW THIS IS NO DIFFERENT. A NATURAL NEXT STEP.
THANKS. I OWE YOU.

WE HAVE NO OTHER CHOICE!

KLAK
KLAK
カラカラ

I'M TAKING REVENGE FOR MY GARMA!

OKAY, GOT IT!
THAT SOUNDED GREAT!
パタン
POMPF
ICELINA ESCHONBACH'S VOICE ACTOR
KEIKO HAN
THANK YOU VERY MUCH.
ガチャ
KCHK
YOUR ROLE ENDING THIS WEEK TOO?

I'M GETTING CANNED NEXT WEEK.

NO MORE APPEARANCES FOR CHAR AZNABLE.

I THOUGHT HE WAS GREAT. I PUT EVERYTHING I HAD INTO THE ROLE.

BUT THE SPONSORS AREN'T FANS OF GUYS IN MASKS.

SHRK

SOUNDS LIKE THE RATINGS ARE IN THE PITS, TOO. GUESS THE SERIES ISN'T LONG FOR THIS WORLD.

HEH! I BET ON THE WRONG HORSE.

SWIG

YOINK

NOW, NOW, CAPTAIN.

ALCOHOL ISN'T GOOD FOR YOU.

CAPTAIN?

CHAR'S A LIEUTENANT.

OH MY, YOU'RE RIGHT. WHATEVER MADE ME THINK OTHERWISE?

FOR SOME REASON, IT JUST FELT NATURAL TO CALL YOU CAPTAIN.

FARE THEE WELL.
UNTIL WE MEET AGAIN,
CAPTAIN.
...
WEIRD GIRL.
VRRRRM
VRRRM
MANAGER, PLEASE LEAVE MY FRIDAYS OPEN AT THIS TIME UNTIL THE END OF THE YEAR.
WASN'T TODAY YOUR LAST APPEARANCE ON *GUNDAM*?
HUH?
YOU'RE BOOKED SOLID AS IT IS!

I HAVE A FEELING THAT THIS IS HOW IT MUST BE.
WELL... OKAY.
PLEASE.
ブロロロ…
VRRRMM
AFTER THAT...

EPISODE 23 LAUNCHED THE G-PARTS.

THE ADZA APPEARED EPISODE

EPISODE 24, "BLACK TRI-STAR WAS A TOUR DE FORCE THAT INTRODUCED TH EVER-POPULAR DOM.

AND TOMINO'S PLA CONTINUED WITH A SMORGASBORD OF ENEMY ROBOTS, LIK THE GOGG, GRUBLO AND Z'GOK.
RRRNG
RRRNG
HOW-EVER...

D-DIRECTOR!

KLK
RRNG
HELLO-NIPPON SUNRISE!

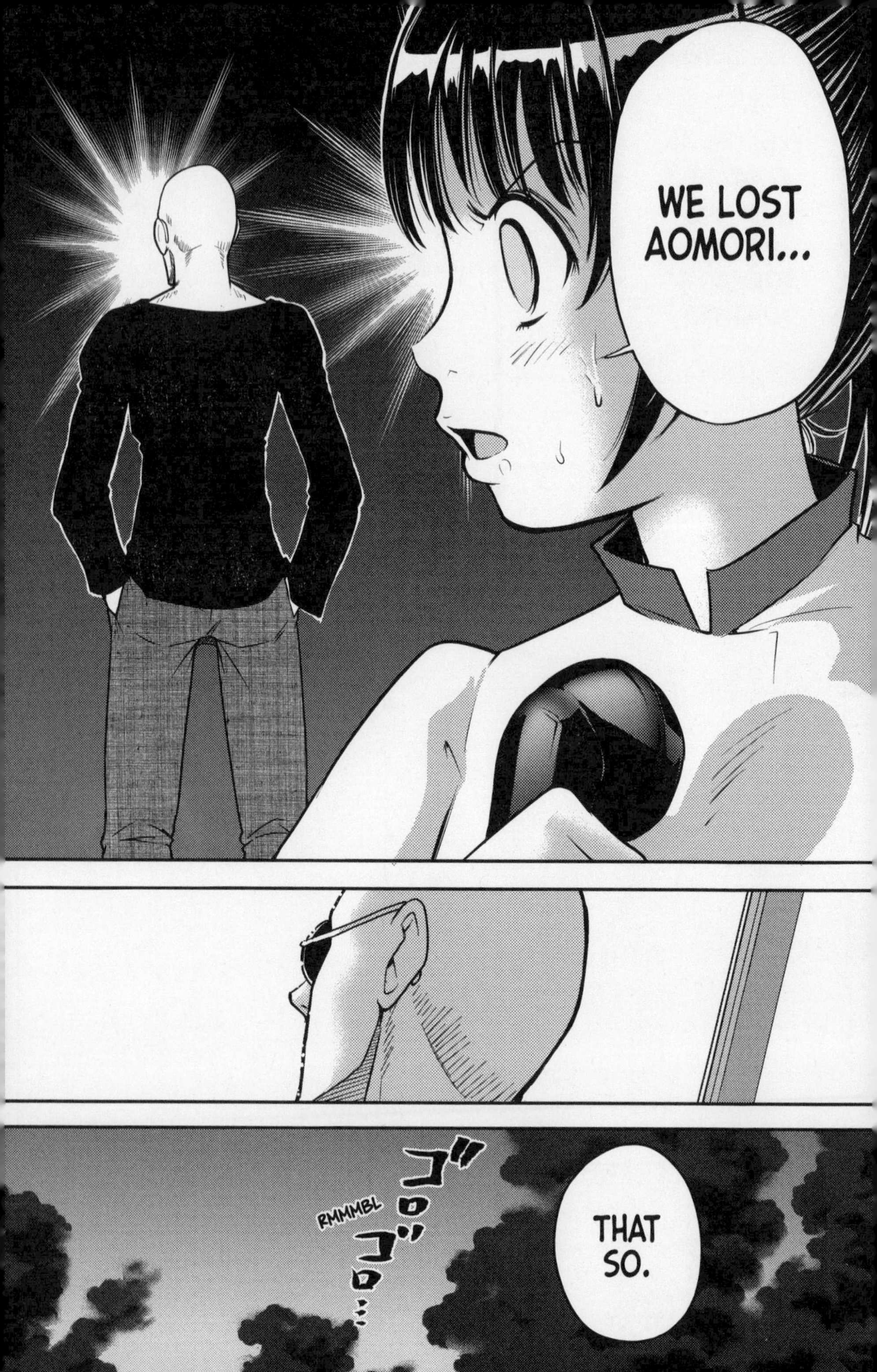
WE LOST AOMORI...
RMMMBL
ゴロゴロ…
THAT SO.

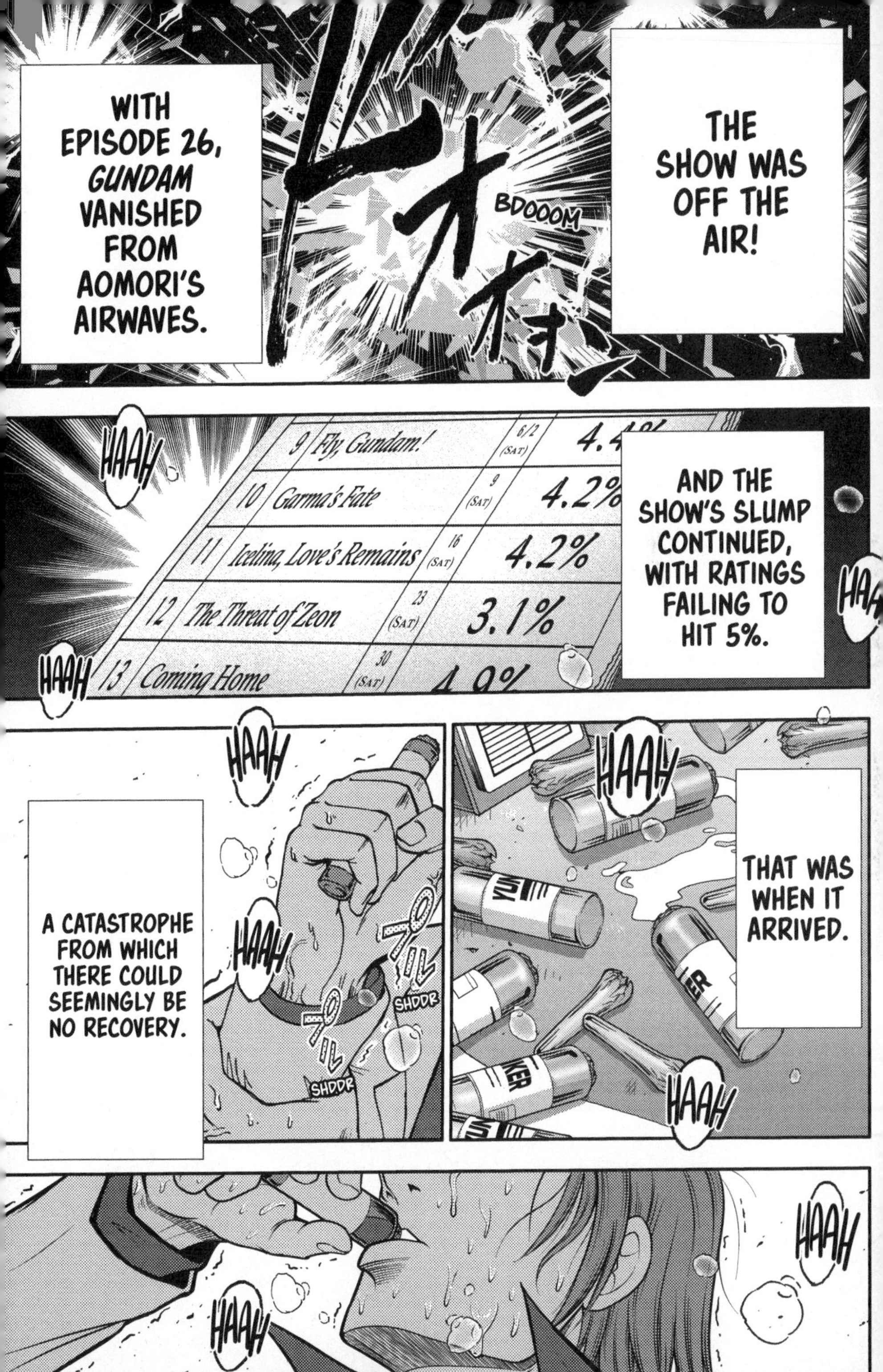

WITH EPISODE 26, GUNDAM VANISHED FROM AOMORI'S AIRWAVES.
BDOOOM
THE SHOW WAS OFF THE AIR!
HAAAH
9 Fly, Gundam! 6/2 (SAT)
10 Garma's Fate 9 (SAT) 4.2%
11 Icelina, Love's Remains 16 (SAT) 4.2%
12 The Threat of Zeon 23 (SAT) 3.1%
13 Coming Home 30 (SAT)
HAAAH
AND THE SHOW'S SLUMP CONTINUED, WITH RATINGS FAILING TO HIT 5%.
HAAAH
A CATASTROPHE FROM WHICH THERE COULD SEEMINGLY BE NO RECOVERY.
HAAAH
SHDDR
SHDDR
HAAAH
THAT WAS WHEN IT ARRIVED.
HAAAH
HAAAH
HAAAH

BSSHOOOM
THUD
Y-YASUHIKO?!
YASUHIKO!!
ゴゴゴゴ…

THE MEN WHO CREATED
GUNDAM

Mechanical Design

Early Zaku design

Mobile Suit Gundam Complete Works, vol. 2

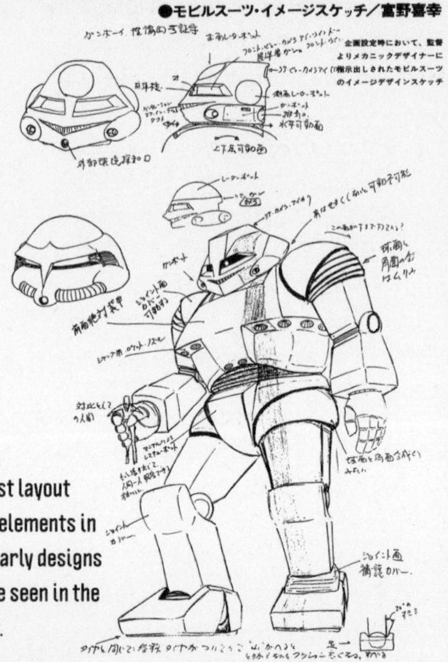

▶ The chest layout and other elements in Tomino's early designs can still be seen in the final draft.

IN THIS STORY, we see the fictional Yoshiyuki Tomino hand Kunio Okawara a design memo for the Zaku. This wasn't embellishment for dramatic effect—this was something the real Tomino actually drew himself.

Though the rough draft is quite different from the finalized version, many of the Zaku's signature design elements are present, including the use of tubing, and the disquieting eye lurking in the head's dark recesses.

Okawara applied his world-class design sensibilities to Tomino's proposal, and the Zaku you see in the upper left is the result. Even at this early stage, the Zaku's defining features are all there, with only minor coloration and design details differing from the final version. The Zaku Machine Gun has its distinctive circular magazine, and the power pipes we know and love are present and accounted for. It was the behind-the-scenes star, in more ways than one.

Note also that the wooden Zaku seen in the story is based on a real-world anecdote. Whenever the actual Kunio Okawara worked on an important mecha design, he would start by crafting a wooden model of it. ◆

Top right: Mobile Suit sketch by Yoshiyuki Tomino

Courtesy of: Sunrise

Ratings

As you saw in the previous chapters, the passion and energy of the hardworking animation team behind *Mobile Suit Gundam* resulted in (sadly) less than impressive ratings. In particular, the broadcast of episode 7 ("The Core Fighter's Escape") earned an audience share of *1.9%*, the lowest out of the entire original airing. Even worse, Episode 26 ("Char's Return") led to the show going off the air in Aomori. Things were looking bleak.

Ratings slightly improved as the show entered its third cour in the fall, but even at its peak, *Gundam* failed to record a double-digit audience share as it careened towards cancellation with episode 43 ("Escape").

When the show was rebroadcast in Tokyo in 1981, however, audiences were aware of *Gundam*, and the show exploded out of the gate with double-digit audience shares. When episode 16 ("Sayla's Agony") aired, it earned a shocking 19.2% share in Tokyo and the surrounding Kanto region. With the films coming out that same year, 1981 was truly the Year of Gundam, leading the show to a second rebroadcast, and firmly cementing its place in anime history. ◆

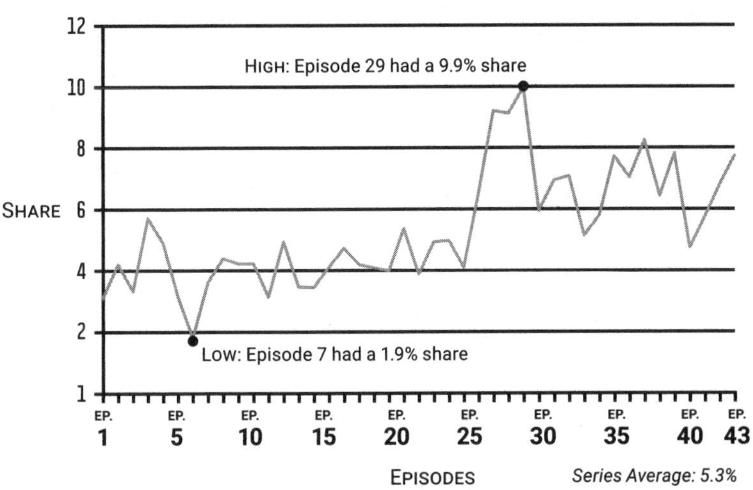

Graph shows the struggle the show experienced and also the potential there was as it "ended."

Courtesy of: Video Research Ltd.

THE MEN WHO CREATED
GUNDAM

EPISODE 7

RESTAURANT AOYAGI

RRRING

RRRING

MR. TOMINO, TELEPHONE CALL FOR YOU.

DON'T THEY KNOW I'M EATING?

KLK

WHAT IS IT?

WE HAVE AN EMERGENCY, SIR.

YASUHIKO, HE... HE...

YEAH? WHAT'D HE DO?

I BEG YOUR PARDON?

RRMMMBBLLL
YASUHIKO COLLAPSED?

RTTL
WE NEED HIM IN THE OPERATING ROOM NOW!
RTTL
RTTL
RTTL
HOW'S THE PATIENT'S CONDITION?!
RTTL
HE'S NOT REGAINING CONSCIOUS-NESS!
RTTL
RTTL
BAAM
DAMMIT, WE HAVE TO HURRY!
NOW OPERATING

AH!

WELL, THAT WAS FAST.
HOW'S YASUHIKO?!
YOU MUST BE THE DIRECTOR... TOMINO, CORRECT?
Y-YEAH.
THERE'S SOMETHING I'D LIKE TO ASK YOU.
WHAT IS IT?

I HEAR MR. YASUHIKO HANDLES TWO THOUSAND KEY FRAMES A MONTH.

IS THAT TRUE?

...

IT IS.

THAT'S UN-BELIEVABLE.

A FIRST-RATE ANIMATOR CAN DO EIGHT HUNDRED A MONTH. A THOUSAND IF THEY'RE TOP-CLASS.

TWO THOUSAND IS UTTER MADNESS.

GLNT

ARE YOU TRYING TO KILL YOUR ANIMATORS?

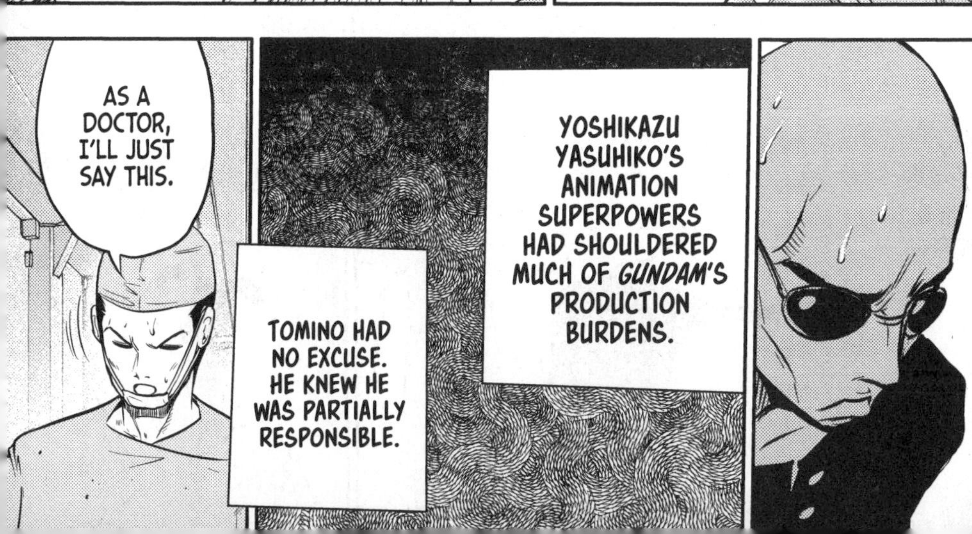

YOSHIKAZU YASUHIKO'S ANIMATION SUPERPOWERS HAD SHOULDERED MUCH OF *GUNDAM*'S PRODUCTION BURDENS.
TOMINO HAD NO EXCUSE. HE KNEW HE WAS PARTIALLY RESPONSIBLE.
AS A DOCTOR, I'LL JUST SAY THIS.

IT ALL HINGES ON TONIGHT.
BEEEP
BEEEP
BEEEP
IT ALL HINGES... ON TONIGHT?
SHOOM
DIREC-TOR?
LET HIM GO.
BUT SIR!

IF YOU'RE NOT A DOCTOR, THERE'S NOT MUCH YOU CAN DO TO HELP.

AND HE'S STILL GOT BROADCAST DEADLINES TO MEET.

THE SHOW MUST GO ON, MISS.

NIPPON SUNRISE

BAM

MR. TOMINO...

WHOA, YOU'RE BACK!

HOW WAS HE?

IS MR. YASUHIKO GONNA BE OKAY?
IS HE SICK?
DIRECTOR!
GRRT

YOU GOD-DAMN IDIOTS!

JOLT

YOU NEED TO WORRY ABOUT YOURSELVES FIRST.

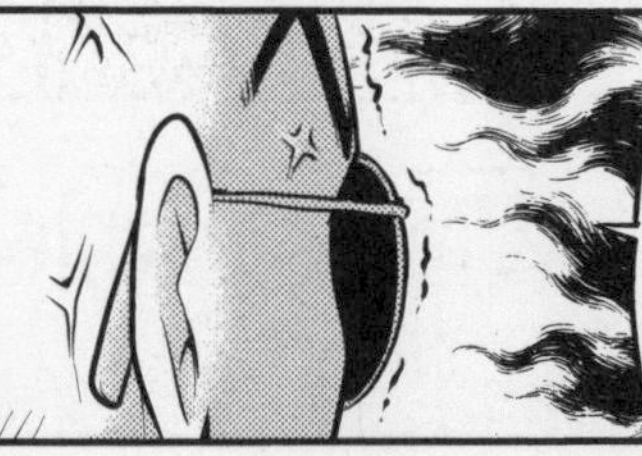

WHO COLLAPSED HERE?

FRIGGIN' YOSHIKAZU YASUHIKO, THAT'S WHO!

ANYONE HERE GONNA COVER THAT GENIUS' WORK?

WELCOME TO HELL ON EARTH, SUCKERS.
GOT IT? THEN GET BACK TO WORK!
ZOOOM
Y-YES-SIR!
WELL, WE'RE SCREWED!
I WONDER IF I'LL EVER GO HOME AGAIN.
NIPPON SUNRISE
CHIRP
CHIRP
CHIRP
CHIRP

WELL, I DON'T SEEM TO BE DEAD.

YOSHIKAZU YASUHIKO SURVIVED THE NIGHT.

HOW-EVER...

OKAY, LET'S TRY A TAKE.

HIS ABSENCE WAS MAKING ITSELF KNOWN.

KLAK
KLAK
HM?
SCENE-24
KLAKA
DIRECTOR, THERE'S NOTHING THERE.

THE HELL THERE ISN'T! TRY OPENING YOUR EYES FOR ONCE!

KLAKA

HUH?

KLAKA

THE BLUE STICK'S AMURO, AND THE RED ONE'S MIRAI.

NOW RECORD THE DAMN LINES!

KLAK

KLAK

THAT'S AMURO?

THE ANIMATORS FELL BEHIND. SOON, PRODUCTION WAS ON THE VERGE OF COLLAPSE.

GUESS THE ANIMATORS ARE STRUGGLING.

GUESS SO! *NYA-HA!*

MRMR

KREE

SIR.

UM...

YEAH, OKAY.

I HAD A FEELING A MEETING WAS COMING.

RMMMBBLLL

THE RATINGS ARE THROUGH THE FLOOR, AS USUAL.
FRANKLY, THEY'RE PAINFUL TO LOOK AT.
THE STUDIO'S IN CHAOS, TOO.
THE SOONER SOMETHING'S DONE, THE BETTER.

WE CAN'T AFFORD TO MISS THE HOLIDAY TOY RUSH, THOUGH.
HOW ABOUT WHEN IT COOLS DOWN? LETS SAY, JANUARY...

HRM. THAT SHOULD WORK.
WE CAN INTRODUCE NEW PRODUCT DURING THE FEBRUARY-AUGUST DOLDRUMS.

YOU HEARD 'EM, TOMINO.
UH, YEAH, BUT...

I HOPE THE NEXT SHOW'S A LITTLE CHEERIER.
YMMR
A CHILD PROTAG, MAYBE?
OOH, YEAH!
YMMR
BETTER TAKE TOMINO OFF THE PROJECT, THEN.

YEAH, IT'S JUST SOME KIDDIE JUNK. WHY ADD DRAMA?
AH HA HA HA HA
ZASHHH
KABUKICHO

BWAHA-HAHA! CHUGA-LUG, BABY!
MAMA, ANOTHER BOTTLE OF CHAMPAGNE!
YOU'RE SO DREAMY, MR. TOMINO!
GRP
GRP

HAVEN'T YOU HAD ENOUGH? YOU'RE IN BAD SHAPE...
YEAH?! WHAT KINDA JERK'S WALKIN' 'ROUND SHINJUKU WITHOUT A LIL' WOBBLE, HUH?!

WHATEVER. I CAN GET SLOSHED ELSEWHERE.
I'M CLOSIN' MY TAB!
WOBBL
SLAM
OH, TOMMY-CHAN...

BAAM

SHIT!

HEY, THE HELL YOU LOOKIN' AT?!

HUH ?!

YOU KNOW WHO THE HELL I AM?!
I DIRECTED GODDAMN *GUNDAM*, YOU-
BLOO-OGH!
WHAM

WHUD
HRGH...
"GUN DAMN?" HEY, YOU HEARD OF THIS SHIT?
SURE HAVEN'T.

GUY'S PROBABLY JUST NUTSO IN THE BRAINO.
SERIOUSLY. NO WAY THAT'S AN ACTUAL SHOW.

I MEAN, NOT LIKE ANYBODY WOULD WATCH IT!
AIN'T THAT THE TRUTH!

GRA-AAA-AH!
ZASSH

ZASHHH

DAMMIT... WHAT'S WITH THE RAIN TODAY?

ON THIS NIGHT IN THE FALL OF 1979...

IT TASTES LIKE BLOOD.

GUNDAM WAS CANCELLED.

EPISODE
8
POLICE STATION
HEAD OF NIPPON SUNRISE
HAJIME YATATE
I'M HERE TO PICK UP YOSHIYUKI TOMINO.
TOMINO? OH, THAT DRUNK FROM LAST NIGHT?
HEY, TIME TO LEAVE.
NO MORE SLEEPING ON THE STREET, OKAY?!
GASP!
KREEK

EPISODE
8

IS THAT REALLY YOSHIYUKI TOMINO?
HE'S A SHADOW OF HIS FORMER SELF.

LIKE AN OLD MAN WHO'S LOST HIS SPARK.

COULD YOU NOT, YATATE?
WE'RE BRINGING HIM WITH US. GET THE CAR.
BRING HIM WHERE?

A BURNT OUT HUSK LIKE HIM ISN'T GOING TO BE ANY GOOD BACK AT THE STUDIO.
HEH

LEMME MAKE A QUICK CALL.
OH?
TKK
TKK

HEY, IT'S ME. YATATE. HUH? NOW?
I'M OUT ON BUSINESS AT THE MOMENT. NAH, NOTHING SERIOUS.

OH YEAH, SO ABOUT THE NEXT SHOW, *TRYDER*...
...

VRRMMMM

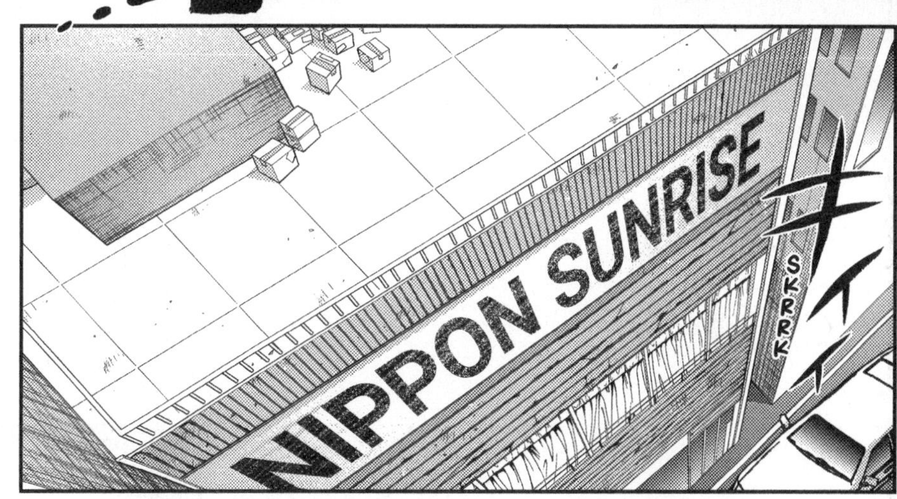

IT'S 5 A.M. NOBODY'S GONNA BE IN THE STUDIO.

STMP

KRRKK

OH MY GOSH...

ROOOOAR
SKRT
SKRT
KRRT
KRRT

KLK

GRRP

RARR
EVERYONE'S STILL HERE!
YOU'RE JOKING, RIGHT?
RARR

AH! IT'S DIRECTOR TOMINO!
HE'S FINALLY BACK!

WE NEED DIRECTION, STAT!

THE SCHEDULE'S SERIOUSLY TIGHT!

AH, THAT'S RIGHT. I STILL HAVEN'T TOLD YOU.

GUNDAM'S FINISHED.

OH, WE KNOW. WE GOT WORD YESTERDAY.

YOU DID? THEN WHY–

IT'S LIKE YOU SAID, DIRECTOR.
YOU'RE GOING TO CHANGE ANIME HISTORY.

SO SHOW US WHAT THAT CHANGE LOOKS LIKE, RIGHT TO THE VERY END!

THERE'S STILL SO MUCH WE WANT TO SEE!

HAH
HAH
YOU DUMB-ASSES.

FINE. I'LL SHOW YOU.
BUT FROM HERE ON OUT, WE'RE HEADING STRAIGHT TO THE 7TH CIRCLE OF HELL.
YOU GOT WHAT IT TAKES TO HANDLE IT?

SUNRISE IS ALREADY HELL ON EARTH, RIGHT?
NYA

WOBBL
PERFECT ...
AH! DIRECTOR!

THEN IT'S FIRE AND BRIMSTONE TIME, FOLKS!
BUT FIRST...
WE'RE GONNA NEED A LITTLE HELP FROM *THEM*.
RMMBBL
YOU DON'T MEAN?
Animec

GOOD MORNING!

WOW, LOOK AT ALL THESE BOXES.

UNSOLD ISSUES, MAYBE?

WHY, IF IT ISN'T TOMINO!

I WOULD HAVE HAPPILY GONE TO SUNRISE IF YOU'D ASKED!

NAH. NOT SOMETHING WE CAN DISCUSS IN KAMI-IGUSA.

HUH?

NEVER MIND.

IS THIS ANIME MAGAZINE THE HELP HE MENTIONED?
THEY SEEM LIKE THEY'RE IN TROUBLE.
CAN THEY REALLY HELP US?

HERE'S THE PROPOSAL FOR THE NEXT SHOW.
POMPF
TRYDER G7.
IT HAS A CHILD PRO-TAGONIST.

AH, TAKING THAT TACK AGAIN TO GET BETTER RATINGS, EH?
AH, SUCH A WASTE, TRULY!
AND TO THINK, WE'VE BEEN MAKING A KILLING!
HUH?!

WAIT. THOSE BOXES... THEY'RE NOT FILLED WITH UNSOLD MAGAZINES?
DON'T BE RIDICULOUS!

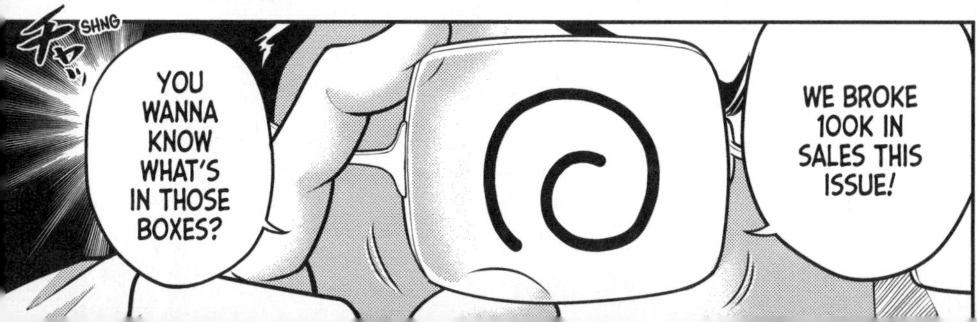
WE BROKE 100K IN SALES THIS ISSUE!
YOU WANNA KNOW WHAT'S IN THOSE BOXES?
SHNG

Animec
POSTCARDS FROM OUR READERS.
EPISODE IMPRESSIONS, FAVORITE CHARACTERS...
ALMOST ALL OF THEM FOR *GUNDAM*.
RMMMBL

FOR GUNDAM!
ALL OF THEM?!
BDOOOM

NYAA
THINGS ARE EVEN CLOSER TO A BOIL THAN I THOUGHT.
INDEED. THE WATER'S A-BUBBLIN'.

ANNOUNCE *GUNDAM*'S CANCELLATION IN THE NEXT ISSUE.
MAKE IT LOUD.

AH HA... SO THAT'S THE GAME.
INNNTERESTING.

OKAY, THEN! YOU WANT LOUD? WE'LL DO LOUD!
CLNK
WE'LL TELL THEM *GUNDAM*'S FAILURE WILL SEND ROBOT ANIME BACK TO THE STONE AGE!
DIRECTOR, THE "HELP" YOU MENTIONED BEFORE, DO YOU MEAN–
YOU'VE SEEN THE MOUNTAINS OF POSTCARDS IN HERE.
THERE'S MAGMA BENEATH JAPAN, AND IT'S STARTING TO BOIL.
IT SCREAMS, "GIMME GUNDAM, DAMMIT!"
RRMMMBBLLL
HELP'S COMIN', ALL RIGHT.
BAM

FROM EVERY VIEWER IN THE COUNTRY!
HE'S BACK!
THAT GLINT IN HIS EYES!
BMDP
THAT VITALITY ROARING UP WITHIN HIM, THREATENING TO EXPLODE!
BMDP
BMDP
THE YOSHIYUKI TOMINO I KNOW, HE'S—
KSHING

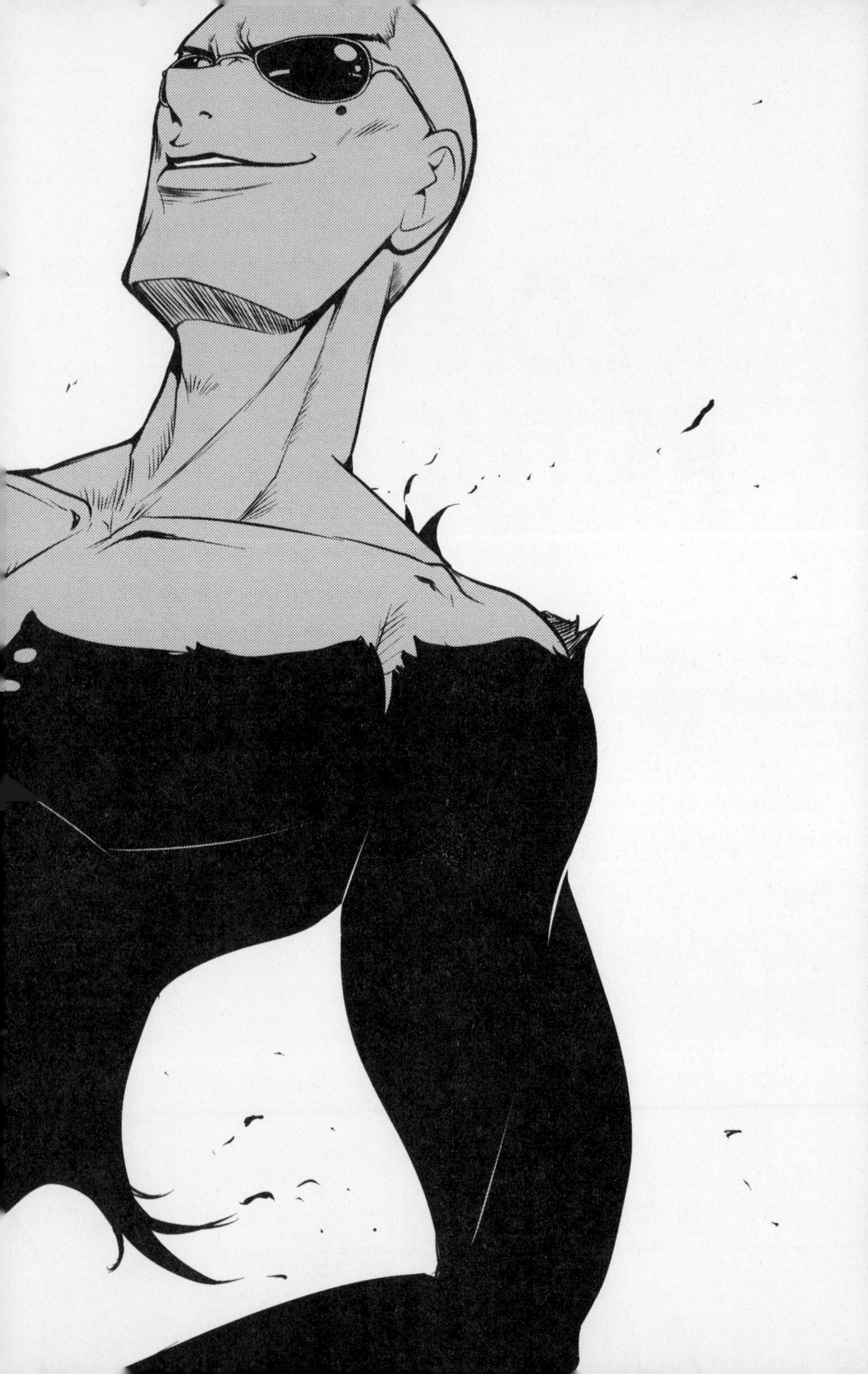

TOMINO
RETURNS!!

RARR
RARR
HEY, WE'RE OUT OF IN-BETWEEN SHEETS!
WHERE'S FRAW BOW'S CHARACTER REFERENCE?!
RMMBL
"SOMETHING UNBELIEVABLE WAS HAPPENING."
MOMOE WAS STRUCK BY A FEELING OF UNEASE
MINGLING WITH ELATION.
BUT THE SCALE OF THE CELEBRATION TO COME
WOULD EXCEED HER WILDEST IMAGININGS.

EPISODE
9

プァー
HONK
プァー
HONK

MORNIN'.
ざわ
MRRMR
ざわ
MORNING.

YOU CATCH YESTERDAY'S *LULU, THE FLOWER ANGEL*?
GREAT ANIMATION, RIGHT?

OKAY, THEN...
HM?

OH MY GOD! LOOK AT THIS, SATO!
HUH?

THIS IS INSANE.
GUNDAM'S BEEN—?!

livehouse
Open Gigs
GIG
BAND SIGNUP

WHY THE LONG FACE, KUROSU?

GUNDAM'S BEEN—!

わなわな
TRMBL

GUNDAM?

GUNDAM'S BEEN—!

GUNDAM'S DONE BEEN CANCELLED!

GASP

RRRING

THAT'S RIGHT. IT'LL BE ENDING NEXT YEAR.
RRRING
YES, RIGHT... HELLO?
RRRING
YES, MY SINCERE APOLOGIES.

WHAT'S GOING ON HERE?! THE PHONES HAVE BEEN RINGING ALL MORNING!
HOW ARE WE SUPPOSED TO GET ANY WORK DONE?!
AND WHAT'S THIS *GUNDAM* THING, ANYWAY?!
10
tv asahi
テレビ朝

NIPPON SUNRISE
DIRECTO
RARR
RARR
RARR
OH, THERE YOU ARE!
DASHH
DIRECTOR TOMINO!
SIR-
WHOA!

RMMMBBL
YEAH?!

EEEK! THERE'S A YAKUZA IN THE BUILDING! A YAKUZA INFILTRATED SUNRISE!
OH NO, OH MY

GET IT TOGETHER, KUSAKARI!
THAT'S DIRECTOR TOMINO!
HUH?!
S-SORRY, I GOT CARRIED AWAY.
WHADDAYA WANT? MAKE IT QUICK!

RARR
RARR
THE TV STATION CALLED.
THEY'RE DEMANDING TO TALK TO THE PERSON IN CHARGE.
SOUNDS LIKE THEY'VE GOT AN EMERGENCY OF THEIR OWN...

ZINGG

DO THEY HAVE ANY IDEA HOW BUSY WE ARE?!

RRMMMBL

SNAPP

THEY'RE THE ONES WHO CANCELLED THE DAMN SHOW!

WIPE YOUR OWN ASSES, YOU SLOBBERING BOOB TUBE SONS OF BITCHES!

YEAH. TELL 'EM THAT.
UH, OKAY...

HUH?
MR. TOMINO, WHAT ARE YOU DOING?

WHAT, YOU CAN'T TELL? YOU'RE A PRODUCTION ASSISTANT, AREN'T YOU?
I'M DRAWING KEY FRAMES!

S-SERIOUSLY?!
THIS IS THE ONLY TIME YOSHIYUKI TOMINO WOULD EVER DRAW KEY ANIMATION FOR *GUNDAM*.
THAT'S JUST HOW BUSY THE STUDIO WAS.

RRRRING
DAMMIT, I TOLD YOU, I'VE GOT NOTHING TO-
THD
QUITE THE GREETING, TOMINO.
SOUNDS LIKE YOU'VE MADE A FULL RECOVERY.
WELL, IF IT ISN'T MR. PRESIDENT.
RARR
RARR
LET ME GUESS, THE TOYS AREN'T SELLING?
RARR
NOT SELLING? HAHAHA, DON'T BE RIDICULOUS.
HUH?

GWAHAHAHAHA
WHY, THEY'RE SELLING LIKE HOTCAKES!
THE GUNDAM DX COMBINER SET IS A HUGE HIT!
A BIG HIT...?
THAT G-ARMOR CRAP I COOKED UP LAST MINUTE... IS SELLING?
BOOOM
THE GUNDAM DX COMBINER SET HAD BECOME ONE OF THE BEST-SELLING TOYS OF 1979!
THE STORY THAT *GUNDAM*'S TOYS SOLD SO BADLY THEY DROVE THEIR MANUFACTURER OUT OF BUSINESS IS A TOTAL FABRICATION.
IN FACT, 1979 WAS THE COMPANY'S MOST PROFITABLE YEAR AND IT WAS ALL THANKS TO *GUNDAM*.

BY THE WAY, TOMINO, I WANTED TO ASK YOU SOMETHING.

YOU WOULDN'T BE ABLE TO EXTEND *GUNDAM*'S BROADCAST, WOULD YOU?

I KNOW THEY DECIDED TO CANCEL IT, BUT STILL.

CAN YOU THINK OF SOME-THING?

YOU'RE ASKING THE IMPOSSIBLE, PREZ.

HELL, EVEN IF WE DID HAVE THE OPPORTUNITY

WE DON'T HAVE TIME TO REWORK THE STORY AT THIS POINT.

YOU-KNOW-WHO'S NOT HERE.

I SEE. YES, I SUPPOSE YOU'RE RIGHT.

SORRY, I WAS BEING UNREASONABLE.

HEHEH... YOU KNOW, EVEN I'VE FOUND MYSELF WONDERING HOW THE STORY'S GOING TO END.

YOU TOLD ME STORIES HAD TO COME FIRST.

YOU WERE RIGHT.

YOU WIN THIS ONE, TOMINO.

NOW THAT'S A COMPLIMENT.

LATER.

CHNG

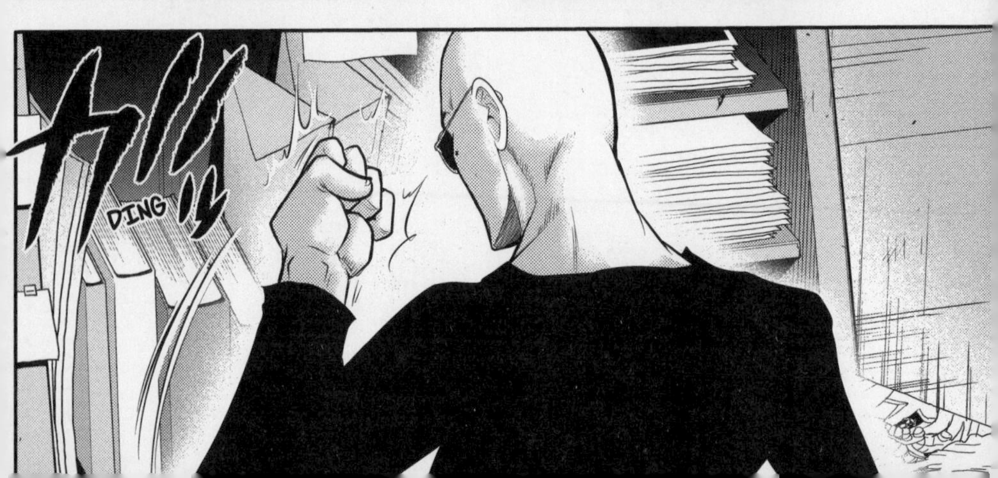

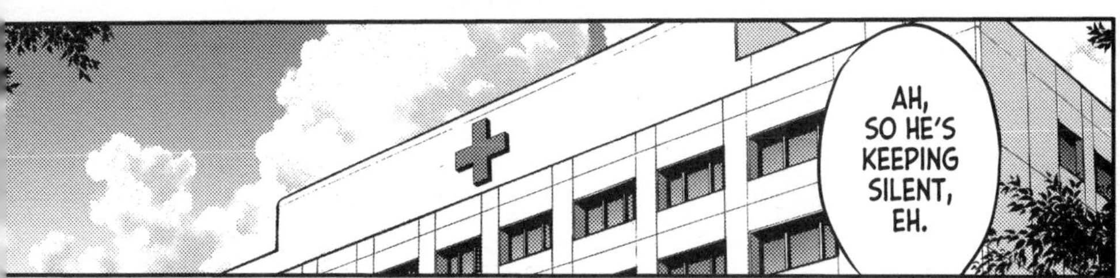
AH, SO HE'S KEEPING SILENT, EH.

HEH. IT'S CERTAINLY VERY TOMINO.
I DON'T LIKE IT. A DIRECTOR SHOULD SAY SOMETHING AFTER THEIR SHOW GETS CANCELLED. COMMON COURTESY!
TCH
NOT QUITE.
HUH?

HE SHOUTED THE CANCELLATION FROM THE ROOFTOPS. NOW IT'S RADIO SILENCE.

HE'S STARVING OUT THE AUDIENCE. LEAVING THEM HUNGRY FOR MORE.

YEAH? FOR WHAT?

THE SHOW'S ALMOST OVER!

GOOD QUESTION. I DON'T KNOW WHAT TOMINO'S THINKING.

THAT SAID,

THINGS HAVE BEEN SET IN MOTION.

NO DOUBT ABOUT IT.

HUFF
HUFF

VIDEO GAMES AND CARD GAMES DIDN'T EXIST YET, SO KIDS WERE BASICALLY THE ONLY TOY STORE CLIENTELE.

WH-WHAT DO YOU WANT?

HENCE THE OWNER'S SURPRISE.

I'D LIKE THE GUNDAM DX COMBINER SET, PLEASE.

HUH?

I'VE GOTTA BUY IT!

***GUNDAM'S* ENDING!**

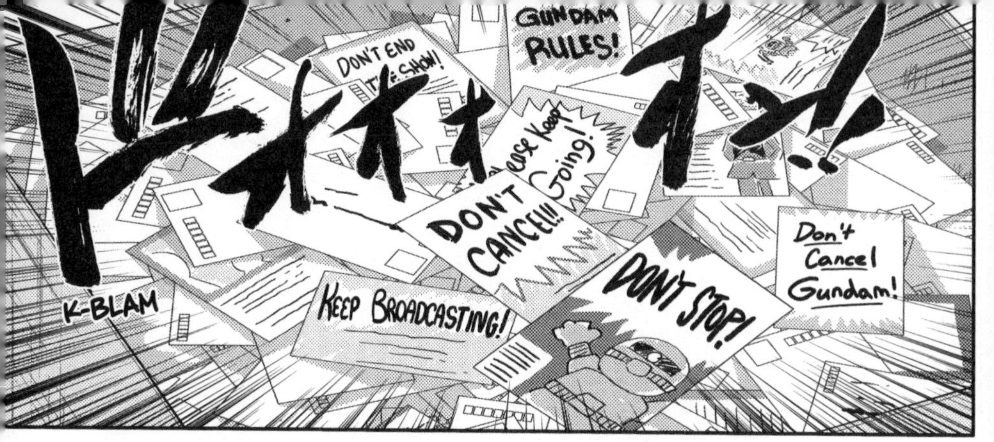
K-BLAM
GUNDAM RULES!
DON'T END
Keep Going!
DON'T CANCEL!!
Don't Cancel Gundam!
DON'T STOP!
KEEP BROADCASTING!

TH-THESE ARE ALL POSTCARDS SENT IN OPPOSITION TO THE SHOW'S CANCELLATION?
YEP!
EVEN MORE IF YOU COUNT PHONE CALLS AND TELEGRAMS! YOU GOTTA DO SOMETHING!

THE POWER OF THE VIEWERS IS ON OUR SIDE.

OKAY, I GET IT NOW...
SHDDR
SHDDR
わな
THE POWER DIRECTOR TOMINO MENTIONED...

I'VE GOTTA BUY IT!

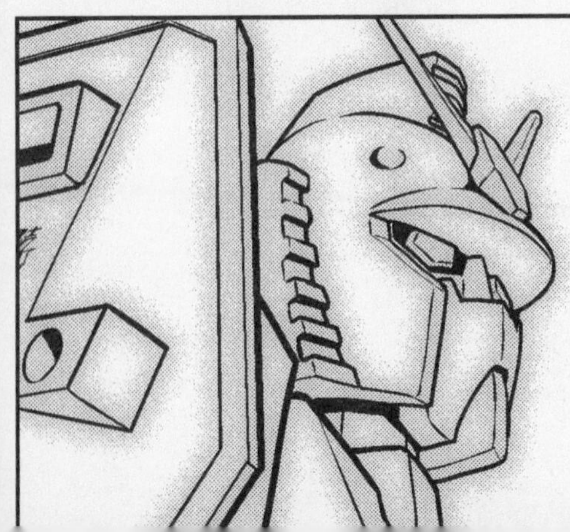

THIS IS WHAT HE WAS TALKING ABOUT!

THE MEN WHO CREATED
GUNDAM

Coffee & Restaurant Aoyagi

Aoyagi as it appeared at the time. The restaurant was renovated to its current look in 1999.

▼ Tomino would often hold meetings with staff using the rear tables seen in the photo to the right.

EARLIER IN THE story, you saw Tomino holding a staff meeting at Coffee & Restaurant Aoyagi, and as it turns out, this is a real cafe that's still open today. Located right beside Kami-Igusa station, visitors to the cafe will find themselves greeted by none other than Sgt. Keroro in the display window—a perfect fit for Sunrise's hometown. And when Aoyagi's 50th anniversary rolled around in 2014, Sunrise staff were there to celebrate in person.

Originally decorated in a brick walled orthodox cafe style, Tomino and the crew would often sit in the back for meetings—and to enjoy a cup of coffee and a bite to eat, of course. Though Aoyagi presently maintains operating hours from 10 a.m. to midnight, it used to stay open until 2 a.m., making it a godsend for hungry, sleep-deprived animators in an era without convenience stores or fast food. The walls are also lined with autographs from local manga authors, cementing its credentials as a hotspot for overworked artists.

Though renovations have changed the atmosphere somewhat, the menu is virtually identical to 1979, offering popular fare like hamburger steak and ginger pork. (Tomino himself often ordered the wagyu steak plate.) If you're ever in the area, why not stop by after visiting the *Gundam* monument in front of Kami-Igusa station? ◆

Courtesy of: Coffee & Restaurant Aoyagi

Gundam DX Combiner Set

During *Gundam*'s original broadcast, the show's toy sponsor, Clover, released this, the Gundam DX Combiner Set. Earlier in the book, you saw fans buy these sets in order to support the show, but they were actually only a part of Clover's main *Gundam* toy line.

Designed as toys first and foremost, the *Gundam* that appears in the set is something of a redesign, with a tremendous level of polish that shows Clover's commitment to detail, but it's undeniably a far cry from the design seen in the show. Intended as a holiday gift item with a higher price point to match, teenage fans who wanted something faithful to the source material couldn't help but notice that something was off.

In order to bring the machines from the show to life, these older fans would have to settle for customizing *Gundam* erasers, which were accurate to the designs in the show, or even creating their very own models. When Gunpla arrived, they were ready and waiting to make it a bona fide phenomenon. ◆

Mobile Suit Gundam DX Combiner Set

▲ A TV show sponsor's greatest strength is its ability to bend the rules... as seen here. An excellent toy, with superb play value.

Courtesy of: Koji Igarashi (Tarkus, Inc.), KK Bestsellers ***Katare! Kidou Senshi Gundam***

THE MEN WHO CREATED
GUNDAM

EPISODE
10
ワー
RARR
IS CUT 45 DONE?!
ガリガリ
SKRCH
SKRCH
ワー
RARR
FINISHED!
ワー
RARR
カリカリ
CHK
CHK
ガリ
CHK
ガリ
CHK
キュ
SKRCHA

EPISODE
10
I'M... DONE...

TIME FOR A QUICK NAP...
ヨロ...
WOBBL
カクッ
WHUMP
JANUARY 1980

THE KEY ANIMATION FOR *MOBILE SUIT GUNDAM* WAS COMPLETE.

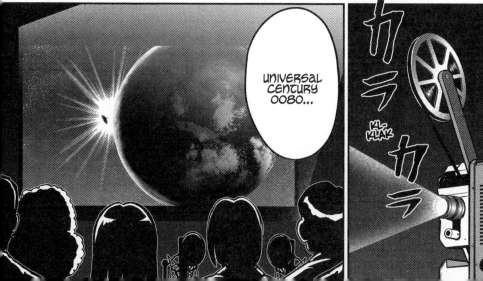

カラ
KL-KLAK
カラ

UNIVERSAL CENTURY 0080...

FOLLOWING THIS BATTLE,

THE EARTH FEDERATION GOVERNMENT AND THE PRINCIPALITY OF ZEON AGREED TO A CEASEFIRE.

KLAK カラ

KLAKA カラ

SHING パッ

IT'S OVER.

A JOB WELL DONE, EH?

GLOMP

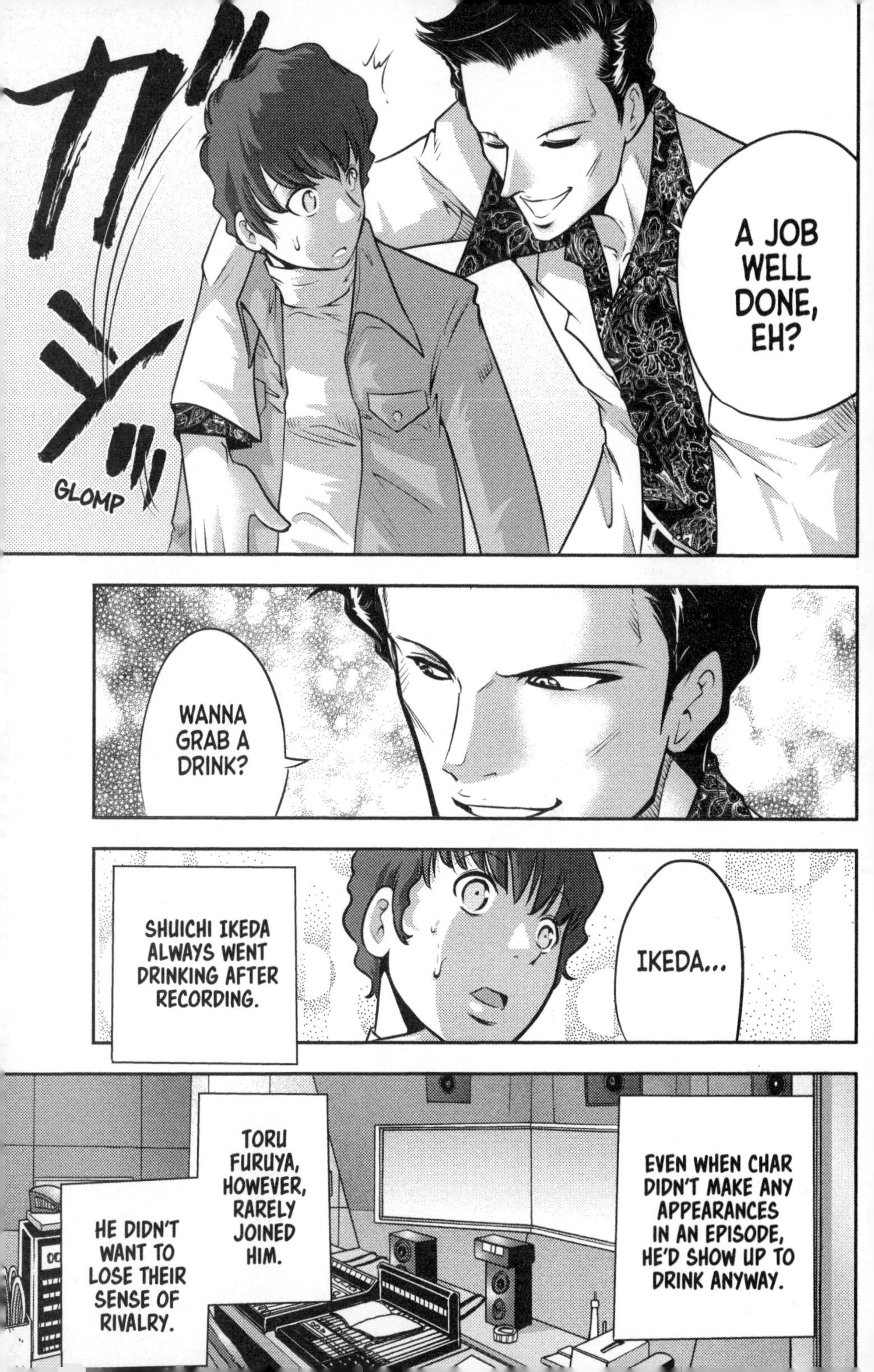

WANNA GRAB A DRINK?

IKEDA...
SHUICHI IKEDA ALWAYS WENT DRINKING AFTER RECORDING.

EVEN WHEN CHAR DIDN'T MAKE ANY APPEARANCES IN AN EPISODE, HE'D SHOW UP TO DRINK ANYWAY.
TORU FURUYA, HOWEVER, RARELY JOINED HIM.
HE DIDN'T WANT TO LOSE THEIR SENSE OF RIVALRY.

IKEDA UNDERSTOOD THAT AND HAD NEVER INVITED HIM OUT TO THE BARS... UNTIL NOW.
SURE!
I'D BE HAPPY TO!

CARE TO JOIN US, HANNY?
PROBABLY NOT GONNA SEE EACH OTHER FOR A WHILE.
HEE HEE ...

WE'LL MEET AGAIN, SOONER THAN YOU KNOW.

WUH?

BE WELL, CAPTAIN.

I DO NOT GET WHAT HER DEAL IS.

YEAH...

機動戦士
ガンダム
MOBILE SUIT GUNDAM
CEASEFIRE CEREMONY WRAP PARTY
PRIVATE PARTY TODAY
ざわ
MRRMR
ざわ
MRRMR

THANKS FOR ALL YOUR HARD WORK OVER THE PAST YEAR, EVERYONE!

AND WHAT A YEAR THAT WAS, RIGHT?

I THOUGHT I WAS GONNA DIE!

WITHOUT FURTHER ADO, DIRECTOR TOMINO IS GOING TO START US OFF BY GIVING A TOAST!

ワー
RAHH
ワー
RAHH

GLARE
URK!
PTOO
LOOK AT YOU CHUMPS.

B-TIER ANIMATORS.
B-TIER IN-BETWEENERS.
B-TIER BACKGROUND ARTISTS.

AND A C-TIER PRODUCTION ASSISTANT!
ZING

WHEN PRODUCTION HALTED AFTER YASUHIKO COLLAPSED, I FIGURED WE WERE UP THE CREEK.
OUR PROJECT SHOULD HAVE IMPLODED.
BUT IT DIDN'T.

AND THE FINISHED PRODUCT IS OUT OF THIS GODDAMN WORLD.

I'M GLAD I GOT TO WORK WITH YOU.

CHEERS, EVERYONE!

CHEERS!

KLNK

BWAHA-HAHA! NOW DRINK UP!
FWOOM
EEEEEK!
MAMA, SAY SOME-THING! THE DIRECTOR'S HAD TOO MUCH TO DRINK AGAIN!
HEE HEE ...
THIS ISN'T LIKE LAST TIME.
HE'S DRINKING WITH JOY IN HIS HEART.
AH HA HA HA HA
AH HA HA
TONIGHT'S BOOZE MUST BE SWEET INDEED, MY DEAR TOMMY...
A FIRE HAD BEEN LIT IN NAGOYA, AS WELL.

THERE, THE FINAL EPISODE, "ESCAPE," HAD AN AUDIENCE SHARE OF 16.5%! AND UNBELIEVABLY, IT REGISTERED A H.U.T.* OF 33.2%!
FOR AN EVENING SHOW, THIS WAS TRULY STAGGERING.

*Note: H.U.T.: Homes using television. The percentage of TV-equipped homes watching a given show.

FANCLUBS SPRANG UP ACROSS THE COUNTRY, THEIR NUMBERS ONLY GROWING IN THE WAKE OF THE LAST EPISODE.

FEATURE: MOBILE SUITS

DOUJIN FANZINES STARTED APPEARING AS WELL, WITH COVERS AGLOW WITH ENTHUSIASM.

FWOOMP

TP
THE NUMBERS ARE GOOD NOW.
TP
SHF
FANS ARE BUYING TOYS AND MERCH IN DROVES.
YOU SAW THE MOUNTAINS OF POST-CARDS, YEAH?

WE'RE AWARE OF THE RATINGS.
NUMBERS ALONE DON'T TELL THE FULL STORY.
WE'RE NOT SURE THINGS ARE GEARED TOWARDS PROFITABILITY.

SHNK
THEY'RE NOT.
THAT'S WHY I BROUGHT MY NEW SPONSOR.
WHAT ?!
WE'RE SMITTEN WITH GUNDAM, REALLY.
SHFF
BANDAI MODEL DEPT. SHIRO KYODA
TRULY, IT IS NO MERE ANIME SERIES.
WE'RE IN THE TOY BUSINESS, LIKE KUROBA. TO AVOID OVERLAP, WE WERE THINKING OF INTRODUCING A PLASTIC MODEL LINE.
WE HOPE YOU'LL ALLOW US TO ASSIST AS A FELLOW SPONSOR!
A NEW SPONSOR JOINING A SHOW AFTER IT FINISHED AIRING WAS UNTHINKABLE.
AND WITH NEW PRODUCTS, TOO? COMPLETELY UNHEARD OF.
RRMMMBL
DIECAST MODELS AND PLASTIC MODELS.
DOUBLE THE PRODUCTS.
SSSSS
NOW GO ON. SAY IT.

WHAT ELSE COULD YOU POSSIBLY NEED?

WHEN DID HE HAVE TIME TO FIND A NEW SPONSOR?
HRM...

SHNG...
WELL? WHAT THE HELL ELSE DO YOU WANT?!
THE FANS HAVE BEEN PRESSURING THE TV STATIONS.
PERHAPS IT'S TIME.
K-BOOM
THE SHOW WAS GETTING A REBROADCAST!
IT WOULD START ON MARCH 5, 1980!
A MERE 39 DAYS FROM THE END OF THE FIRST AIRING!

NIPPON SUNRIS
GOSH, THINGS REALLY WORKED OUT!

KIDS WHO STARTED WATCHING AT THE END OF THE SHOW SENT TONS OF POSTCARDS SAYING THEY WANTED TO WATCH FROM THE BEGINNING!
I SURE HOPE LOTS OF PEOPLE END UP WATCHING.
THAT'LL MAKE ALL OUR HARD WORK WORTH IT!

WHAT'S ON THE DOCKET TODAY?

YOU HAVE AN INTERVIEW WITH AN ANIME MAGAZINE.

AN ANIME MAG, HUH.

NIPPON SUNRISE

THANKS FOR TAKING THE TIME TO TALK WITH US TODAY.

THE RESPONSE FROM OUR READERS HAS BEEN INCREDIBLE!

I BET.

IT'S UNFINISHED. NOT EVEN WORTH WATCHING.

U-UN-FINISHED?
REALLY?
YUP.
TOTAL GARBAGE.
YOU'D HAVE TO BE A TOTAL DUMMY TO WATCH IT.

HUH?!
BUT DIRECTOR! JUST LAST NIGHT, YOU TOLD EVERYONE IT WAS OUT OF THIS WORLD!
WHY?!

WHAT'S GOTTEN INTO YOU?!

1980.
BALL
1200
GAME & WATCH
RIGHT
LEFT
EPISODE
11
SHINJUKU KOMA THEATER
THE MASSES REMAINED AT PEACE, BUT THEY SENSED THE DAWNING OF A NEW AGE WAS AT HAND.
サブちゃん
歌謡ショー
地獄の黙示録
NIPPON SUNRISE
RRMMBL
A WAVE HAD RIPPLED FORTH FROM A STUDIO IN KAMI-IGUSA, ON TOKYO'S WESTERN OUTSKIRTS.
IT HAD STARTED SMALL, BUT SOON IT WOULD ENGULF ALL OF JAPAN!
BOOOOM

EPISODE 11

ゴゴゴゴ…
RRMMMBBL

DIRECTOR TOMINO?
WHAT THE HECK ARE YOU THINKING?

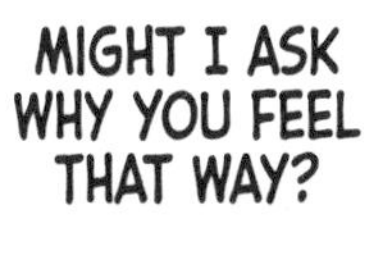

GUNDAM IS UNFINISHED?
MIGHT I ASK WHY YOU FEEL THAT WAY?

POOMPF
ポフ
6/14/XX (initially conceptualized)
Juaggu
very extreme weapon
Acguy-Type
We think this might be going too far.
THESE ARE MY GUNDAM NOTES.
SHF
ジュボ
CALL IT THE TOMINO MEMO.
THE "TOMINO... MEMO?"
ペラ
FLP
Mobile Armor
Zam
Green
Grey
Gundam
MOTHER OF GOD!

A SECRET MEETING BETWEEN SAYLA AND DEGWIN ZABI?
KUSCO AL, ANOTHER NEWTYPE PILOT?
A BATTLE FOR GRANADA ON THE MOON? ...WHERE CHAR KILLS KYCILIA?!
GIHREN LAUNCHING IN HIS OWN MS TO FACE AMURO ONE-ON-ONE?!

M-M-M-MISTER TOMINO!
WHAT IS THE MEANING OF THIS?!

GUNDAM GOT CANCELLED. YOU KNOW THIS.

ホワ POOF

WE BASICALLY HAD TO TEAR OUT THE ENDING.

MAN, IF ONLY WE GOT TO DO THE FULL RUN! WE WERE GONNA INCLUDE SO MUCH COOL SHIT!

IF ONLY THE VIEWERS COULD SEE IT ALL!

PLUS, THE SPACE ARC DIDN'T INCLUDE A SINGLE DRAWING BY YASUHIKO.
IF THAT AIN'T UNFINISHED, I DON'T KNOW WHAT IS.
FLP
FLP
I SEE...
SURE HOPE WE GET TO SEE THIS SOMEDAY.

AHAHA! NOT HAPPENIN'!
WE'RE NOT GETTING ANOTHER TV SEASON.
AND WE'D NEVER MAKE MONEY SELLING IT ON SUPER 8.

PHOOO
IT'D HAVE TO BE A MOVIE.

A MOVIE?!

YEP.

AND NOT JUST A COMPILATION, EITHER. THAT'D BE BORING.

KSH

WE'D HAVE NEW SCENES ALL OVER THE PLACE!

THWD

WITH YASUHIKO REDRAWING TONS OF IT!

AW, MAN!

WHAT I'D DO TO MAKE *THAT* HAPPEN!

RMMMMBL

Animemo
MOBILE SUIT GUNDAM SPECIAL!!
from the Show
BSHOOOOOM
A GUNDAM MOVIE?!
IN FOUR PARTS?!
WITH A RUNTIME OVER 10 HOURS?!
Animemo
MOBILE SUIT GUNDAM SPECIAL!!

OKAWARA DESIGNS
SPECIALIZING IN MECHANICAL DESIGNS
☎(12)3456
KLANG
I'D NEVER EVEN HEARD OF THAT MEMO,
SKRRREEE
AND I'M THE PRODUCTION ASSISTANT.
HE WAS ALREADY PREPARED FOR THE NEXT STEP.
HEH.
I DON'T THINK SO, MISS.
THAT FINAL EPISODE WAS A MIRACLE.
SHKK
OKAWARA DESIGNS
OKAWARA DESIGNS
THAT MEMO'S PROBABLY JUST A ROUGH OUTLINE.
SKREEE
HUH?

OKAWARA DESIGNS
SHKK
MAD GENIUS YOSHIYUKI TOMINO AND A ROOM OF BRILLIANT SCRIPT-WRITERS
PUT IN SLEEPLESS NIGHTS CRAFTING THAT.
THEY DIDN'T HAVE MUCH TIME,
BUT THEY BUILT THAT THING WITH PAINSTAKING PRECISION.
SHREEEE
THERE'S NO IMPROVING ON A SCRIPT LIKE THAT.
HE'S PROBABLY THINKING THE SAME.
OF THAT, I CAN ASSURE YOU.
TH- THEN...
WHY DID HE SAY ALL THAT STUFF?

THOSE WERE *MAGIC WORDS* HE USED.

MAGIC WORDS?
YEAH.
WHEN YOU SAY YOU'RE MAKING A MOVIE... THAT HAS POWER.

IT'S JUST AN IDEA AT THIS POINT, BUT THE WORD "MOVIE" INSPIRES NONETHELESS.

LIKE I SAID, MISS. MAGIC.

FWSH

K-KLANG

カランカラン

WELCO—

EEEGH!

I'D LIKE ANOTHER GUNDAM DX COMBINER SET, SIR!
MAGIC ENOUGH TO MOVE PEOPLE TO ACTION.
KLUNK

HRK!
TO WITNESS YOSHIKAZU YASUHIKO'S ARTISTIC BRILLIANCE IS TO BE STUNNED SILENT.
SHWP
すっ
WITHOUT DRAWING SKETCHES, HIS BRUSH WOULD SUDDENLY TAKE TO THE PAGE
SHWSH
RACING ACROSS ITS SURFACE WITH SPEED AND BEAUTY.

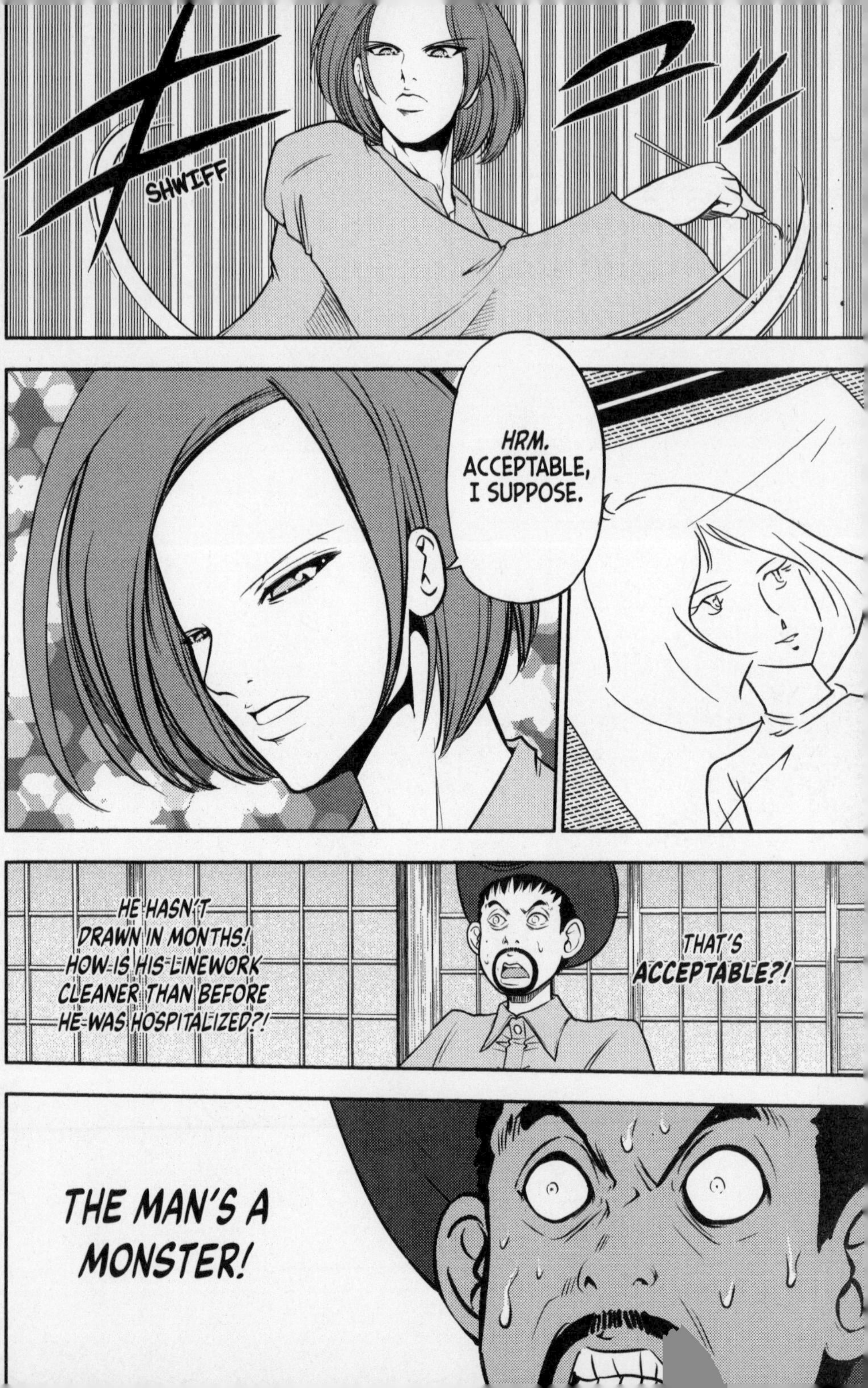

SHWIFF

HRM. ACCEPTABLE, I SUPPOSE.

THAT'S ACCEPTABLE?!
HE HASN'T DRAWN IN MONTHS! HOW IS HIS LINEWORK CLEANER THAN BEFORE HE WAS HOSPITALIZED?!

THE MAN'S A MONSTER!

YASUHIKO RETURNS!

FWOOOOSH

NOW, THEN.

THE PLAYERS HAVE ASSEMBLED!

EPISODE
12

NIPPON SUNRISE
BAAM
Animemo
March
FMS Encyclopedia
Spring Anime Guide
Everything GUNDAM!
Studio Visit
How Gundam Was Made
Fan Meetup Report
Spring Anime Creator Interview
Anime Club
EBOOK
YOUR TOP 5 SCENES
GUNDAM
Federation Vs. Zeon War Chronicle
WOW!
THE ANIME MAGS ALL HAVE *GUNDAM* ON THE COVER!
OH MY GOSH, THE FEATURES ARE ALL ABOUT *GUNDAM* TOO—
FLP
YEAH, AND THE SHOW'S OVER! CRAZY, RIGHT?

BAAAAM
WOAH!

WH-WH-WHAT THE HECK?!
SAYLA'S N-N-NAKED!

THE TITLE OF THIS NUDE PINUP WAS "TROUBLED ARTESIA," AND THE MAGAZINE THAT INCLUDED IT ACHIEVED TRULY UNHEARD-OF SALES.
キーコー
SKRK
キーコー
SKRK
SAYLA!
SAYLAAA!
MALE READERS SCOURED BOOKSTORES ACROSS THE NATION IN SEARCH OF COPIES.

ANIME MAGAZINES THESE DAYS SURE ARE SOMETHING.
WHOA!
BAM
GIMME THAT!
GRRAH
THE HELL'S GOING ON HERE?!
KCHA
SOMEONE'S GONNA PAY!
DIRECTOR, LISTEN, I GET HOW YOU FEEL.
BUT BE GENTLE, OKAY?
OUT EDITORIAL SPEAKING.
HEY, IT'S ME! TOMINO!
HUH?!

CAN'T YOU PERVOS DRAW SAYLA ANY SEXIER?!
WUH ?!
LISTEN. I'M A CREATOR TOO, Y'KNOW.
MRRMR
ざわ
BUT THERE ARE SOME LINES YOU JUST DON'T CROSS.
LET ME SPELL IT OUT FOR YOU.

SAYLA'S NIPPLES SHOULD BE *PINK*!

I-IS TOMINO JUST AN IDIOT?
GOT IT?!
KA-SLAM

THE HELL YOU STARING AT?
HUH? OH, UH, NOTHIN'.
JOLT
THEN GET YOUR ASS BACK TO WORK!
S-SIR!
WAUGH!
WAUGH!
WAUGH!
WAUGH!
THIS WOULD COME TO BE KNOWN AS THE *TROUBLED ARTESIA PINUP* INCIDENT.
STILL...
March
MS Encyclopedia
Spring Anime Guide
IF IT'S GETTING THIS HUGE, MAYBE IT'S TIME.
OKAY, I'M HEADING IN!
SHWF
HEADING WHERE?
THE MOVIE COMPANY.

ヒュオオオオォ…
FWOOOOSH
SHOCHIKU
松竹会館

FWOO ♪ HELL OF A BUILDING, INNIT?

UM, SIR? YOU MADE AN APPOINTMENT, RIGHT?
THE HELL WOULD I DO THAT FOR?

HUH ?!

H-HOLD ON, DIRECTOR TOMINO!
MIND IF I MEET WITH THE PRESIDENT?
...
HUH?
RECEPTION

LET HIM KNOW A DIRECTOR OF FINE ANIMATED FILMS IS HERE TO SEE HIM.

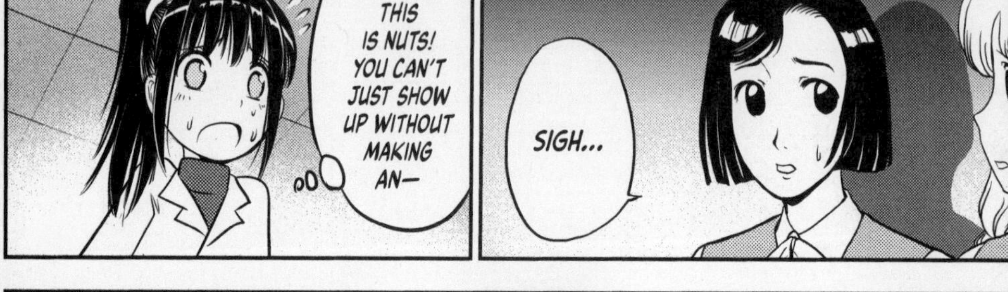

SIGH...
THIS IS NUTS! YOU CAN'T JUST SHOW UP WITHOUT MAKING AN—

THE PRESIDENT HAS AN OPENING. THIS WAY.

WHAT'D I TELL YA?

WUU-UH?!

NO WAY.

TMP

WE'RE IN THE MIDDLE OF THE BIGGEST ANIME BOOM EVER.

TMP

MOVIE GUYS ARE TRIPPING OVER THEMSELVES TRYING TO FIND THE NEXT BIG THING.

GUNDAM REALLY IS AMAZING, HUH?

JUST REALIZING THAT NOW? *HEH.*

PRESIDENT'S OFFICE

BAM

PRESIDENT'S OFFICE

COME IN, COME IN! GOODNESS, I COULD HARDLY BELIEVE IT WHEN I GOT THE CALL FROM RECEPTION.

OKAYAMA, PRESIDENT OF SHOCHIKU.

TOMINO, DIRECTOR AT LARGE.

SO YOU'LL BE MAKING *YAMATO* FOR ME?

OH HOHOHO HO HO

I CAN HARDLY BELIEVE MY LUCK!

Note: At the time, anime was still occasionally referred to as "TV manga" or "manga films," reflecting its lack of acceptance in society at large.

TOEI'S HANDLING DISTRIBUTION FOR *YAMATO*, SIR.

OH? I NEVER COULD KEEP THIS *MANGA* BUSINESS STRAIGHT!

SOMETHING'S OFF HERE...

NO, NOT *YAMATO*! *GUNDAM*, DAMMIT!
THE GUN DAM? WHEREVER MIGHT THAT BE?
SOME-WHERE IN INDONESIA, I THINK.
IT'S NOT A DAM! IT'S A ROBOT ANIME!
THE NAME OF THE ROBOT IS ***GUNDAM***, DAMMIT!
YOU'VE SERIOUSLY NEVER HEARD OF IT?!
A ROBOT ANIME? AH, THAT'S RIGHT, SIR!
THIS IS A VERY POPULAR WAY TO ADVERTISE TOYS!
OH, YES! MY GRANDSON LOVES THE STUFF! CAN'T GET ENOUGH OF IT!
TOMINO HAD HEARD IT BEFORE, AND HE WOULD HEAR IT AGAIN.
"ANIME IS FOR KIDS."

EVEN IN 1980, AWARENESS OF ANIME REMAINED LOW.
THE AVERAGE PERSON WOULD NEVER BE ABLE TO DISCERN BETWEEN *YAMATO* AND *GUNDAM*.
SHING
GUNDAM HAD BECOME A BREAKOUT HIT, CERTAINLY.
HOWEVER,
IT WAS ONLY A HIT BY THE HUMBLE STANDARDS OF A STILL-GROWING INDUSTRY.
SO THAT'S HOW
THE WORLD SEES US.
GUNDAM... GUNDAM...
AH, FOUND IT. CREATED FOR TV, HM?
FLP
NIPPON SUNRISE HANDLED PRODUCTION.
1979

SUNRISE, EH?

MY, WHAT A CUTE LITTLE COMPANY!

BARELY A TENTH THE SIZE OF TOEI, IT LOOKS LIKE.

SIMPLY ADORABLE!

OH HO HO HO

...

TOMINO, MY COMPANY DEALS IN FEATURE FILMS.

MANGA FILMS? ALL VERY CONFUSING, TO BE HONEST.

MORE TO THE POINT, CAN YOU REALLY CALL A MANGA MADE IN YOUR BACKSTREET WORKSHOP A FEATURE?

POMPF

1979 VISUAL WORKS LIST

HOHOHO!

DON'T MAKE ME LAUGH.

EPISODE 13

TOMINO, IT'S AS WE TOLD YOU.

WHAT WE WANT IS A *YAMATO*.

IF A *YAMATO*'S WHAT YOU'RE GOING TO MAKE, WE CAN TALK.

YOU TRAVELED SO FAR TO GET HERE, AFTER ALL.

...

HOW DOES SOME NICE HOT *BUBUZUKE* SOUND, TOMINO?

EPISODE 13

DON'T DO IT, DIRECTOR!
IF SOMEONE FROM KYOTO OFFERS YOU TEA OVER RICE, THEY WANT YOU TO LEAVE!

BUT THIS *BUBUZUKE* IS PIPIN' HOT! HOW AM I SUPPOSED TO TURN THAT DOWN?!

SHOCHIKU KAIKAN

SO...

NIPPON SUNRISE

YOU TURNED TAIL AND RAN, EH?

BRRAP

SHADDUP! I ATE TEN BOWLS OF THE STUFF!

I'M SURE THEY WERE VERY IMPRESSED

WITH YOUR BRAZEN IDIOCY.

THEY HAD THE NERVE TO ASK FOR *YAMATO*!

THEY DON'T KNOW SHIT ABOUT SHIT!

ARA DESIGNS

THEY DON'T?

I'M NOT SO SURE ABOUT THAT.

SPACE BATTLESHIP YAMATO MADE ¥2 BILLION IN GROSS RECEIPTS.[1] THAT'S A HIT BY ANY MEASURE.

SHOCHIKU PUT OUT TWO TORA-SAN MOVIES[2] THE SAME YEAR, AND YAMATO CRUSHED 'EM.

THEY'RE MOVIE PEOPLE. THERE'S NO WAY THEY MISSED THAT.

Note: [1]$29 million in 2021.
[2]*It's Tough Being a Man* series, a mainstay of Japanese cinema from 1969 to 1997.

AH!

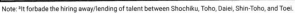

HM, YES, THAT MAKES SENSE.

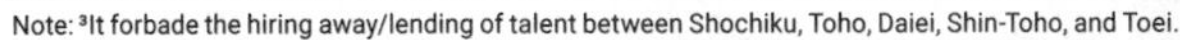

Note: [3]It forbade the hiring away/lending of talent between Shochiku, Toho, Daiei, Shin-Toho, and Toei.

THEY CAN'T MAKE A YAMATO WITHOUT VIOLATING THE FIVE-COMPANY AGREEMENT.[3]

BUT THEY ASKED ME TO DO IT ANYWAY.

SHOCHIKU'S PRESIDENT KNOWS THAT BETTER THAN ANYONE.

PLINK

I GET IT NOW. SO THAT'S HOW IT IS.
YOU'RE A SNEAKY ONE, MR. PRESIDENT.
GRRP
SHAKKK
D-DIRECTOR?
YOU'VE REACHED SHOCHIKU.
YEAH. IT'S ME. TOMINO.
PATCH ME THROUGH TO THE PRESIDENT.
WHY, IF IT ISN'T MR. TOMINO!
HOW CAN I ASSIST YOU?

I WANT YOU TO SEND US ONE OF YOUR MOVIE P.R. GUYS.

BONUS POINTS IF THEY WERE INVOLVED WITH *YAMATO*.

OH? PLANNING SOMETHING BIG?

LET'S REVIEW *YAMATO*'S PATH TO SUCCESS.

BOTH *YAMATO* AND *GUNDAM* ARE SCI-FI ANIME.

BOTH GOT CANNED EARLY BUT HAD COMEBACKS THANKS TO FAN SUPPORT.

THEIR STORIES ARE DIFFERENT, BUT

FROM A BUSINESS STANDPOINT, THEY'RE TWINS.

WHEN YOU ASKED US TO MAKE A *YAMATO*...

YOU WERE ASKING US TO CREATE THE SAME KIND OF BOOM AS *YAMATO!*

AIN'T THAT RIGHT ?!

BAAAAAM

ANOTHER YAMATO BOOM?!

SO THAT'S WHAT HE MEANT!

HOHOHO!

WELL DONE. A BRILLIANT DEDUCTION.

WITHOUT ANIME, JAPAN'S FILM INDUSTRY IS GONNA SHRIVEL UP AND DIE. THE DAY'S COMING.
ゴゴゴゴ…
RRMMMBL
COUNT ON IT.

YOU PROBABLY THINK I'M TALKIN' OUT MY ASS HERE.
I TALK BIG. I'LL FREELY ADMIT THAT.
BUT THIS IS DIFFERENT.
I'VE SEEN IT IN THE STUDIO. LIVED IT.

THIS INDUSTRY'S GOT GENIUSES LIKE YOU WOULDN'T BELIEVE. DAY AFTER DAY, THEY LURK IN THE SHADOWS, BIDING THEIR TIME.
EVERY ONE OF THEM IS TALENTED ENOUGH TO BLOW YOUR BRAINS OUT.

WHEN THEY EMERGE FROM THEIR COCOONS TO SPREAD THEIR WINGS,
THEY'RE GONNA REIGN OVER THE BOX OFFICE, TOP TO BOTTOM.

SO DON'T YOU FRIGGIN' DARE UNDER-ESTIMATE ANIMATORS!

...

RIGHT. I HAVE A SKILLED PROMOTER I CAN ASSIGN.

I TRUST YOU'VE AN ANIME EXPERT ON YOUR END?

WE'VE GOT JUST THE GUY FOR THE JOB.

HE GOT NECK DEEP IN THE *YAMATO* BOOM. PRETTY MUCH RUINED HIS LIFE FOR IT.

RIGHT NOW, HE'S WADING AROUND *GUNDAM*, UP TO HIS EYEBALLS.

Animec

EDITORIAL

ACHOO!

WH-WHO IS IT?

WHO'S TALKING ABOUT ME?

YOU SAID ANIME'S GOING TO REIGN SUPREME AT THE BOX OFFICE.
WHEN IS THAT HAPPENING?
NEXT YEAR.
KA-SLAM
BEEEP
BEEEP

NEXT YEAR?
PLANNING TO OPEN IN 1981, EH?

WE MAY BE PARTNERING WITH A TRULY OUTRAGEOUS INDIVIDUAL, SIR.

S-SO? WHAT'S HAPPENING WITH *GUNDAM*?
GOD ONLY KNOWS.
I'M GONNA PLAY SOME PACHINKO.
HELLO EVERYONE! KYODA HERE, FROM BANDAI!
YO.
I BROUGHT SAMPLES OF OUR NEW PRODUCT!
GUNDAM PLASTIC MODELS! 1/144 SIZE!
BAM
PLASTIC MODELS?
YUP.

HERE'S WHAT THEY LOOK LIKE WHEN YOU FINISH!

AW, LOOK AT THAT! IT'S A CUTE LIL' GUNDAM!

GOODNESS, THEY'RE HIGH QUALITY. THE PROPORTIONS ARE PERFECT.

THE HELL? WHERE'S THE CORE FIGHTER?

NO COLORS, EITHER?!

CUT US SOME SLACK, SIR!

WE'RE SELLING THESE AT ¥300 A POP! WE'RE LIMITED IN WHAT WE CAN DO HERE!

Note: ¥300 = $4.75 in 2021

¥300, HUH. THAT'S PERFECT FOR KIDS.
THEY'LL BE ON CANDY STORE SHELVES SOON.
WE'RE WORKING ON CHAR'S ZAKU RIGHT NOW, TOO.
AS FAR AS ANYONE WAS CONCERNED, THIS WAS JUST ANOTHER PIECE OF GUNDAM MERCH.
HOW-EVER...
DID YOU SAY ZAKU?!
THEY'RE REALLY POPULAR!

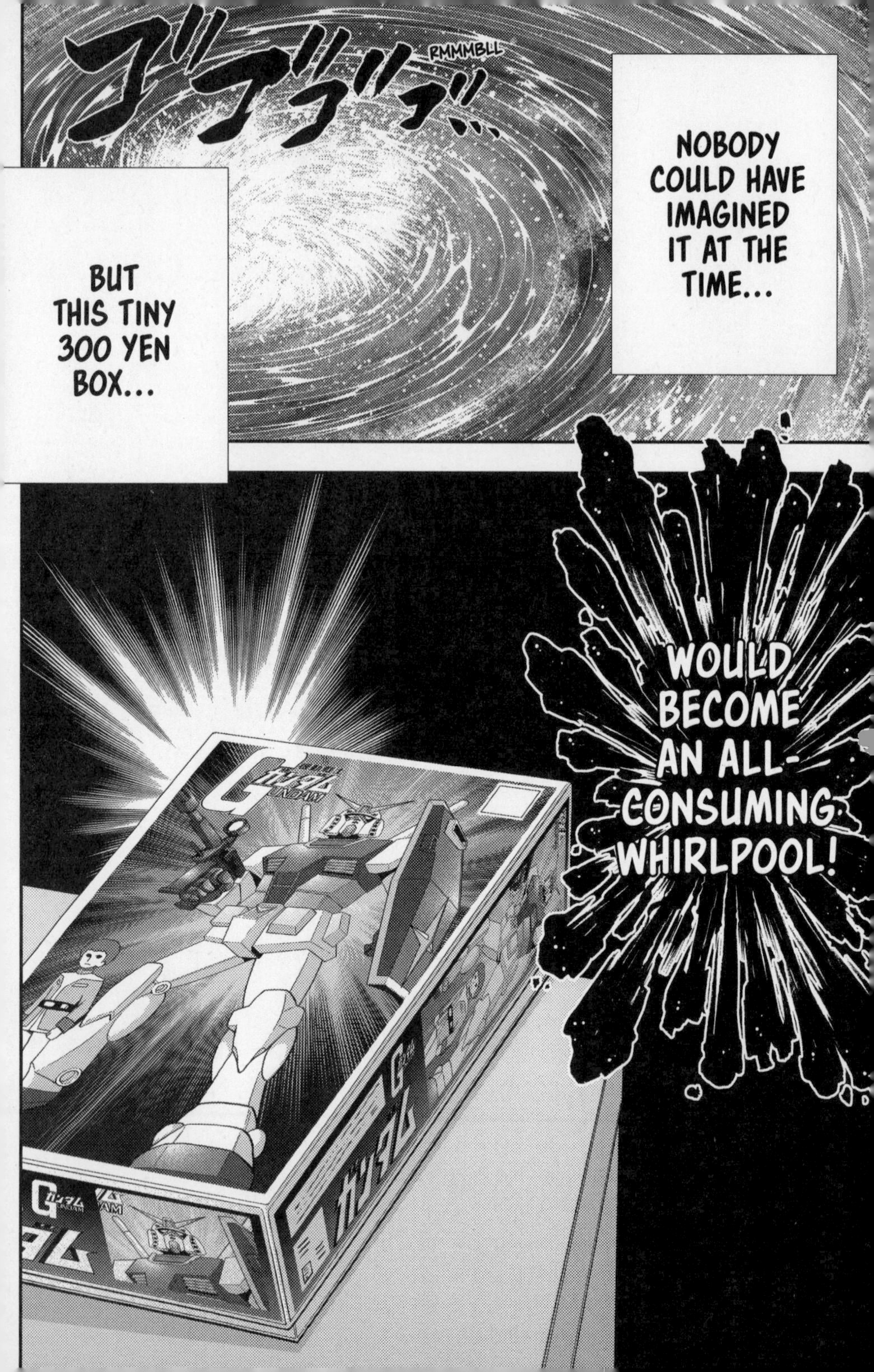
RMMMBLL
NOBODY COULD HAVE IMAGINED IT AT THE TIME...
BUT THIS TINY 300 YEN BOX...
WOULD BECOME AN ALL-CONSUMING WHIRLPOOL!
ガンダム

THE MEN WHO CREATED
GUNDAM

Wrap Party - The Ceasefire Ceremony

EARLIER IN THE story, you saw Yoshiyuki Tomino declare the unthinkable through the pages of *Animec* magazine: *Mobile Suit Gundam*... had been cancelled. It was an announcement that sent shockwaves throughout Japan's anime fandom, and it really happened.

Animec #8, published in 1979, featured an interview in which Tomino relayed the bad news to Masanobu Komaki. The interview goes into detail on the changes made to the show following cancellation, and the struggles Tomino and the team went through once the decision was made. The interview dangles crucial information about mysteries left unsolved, and steps taken to resolve the story. It's hard to imagine reading this as a fan, seeing the possibilities vanishing before your eyes, and not feeling fired up about wanting to save the show.

Following the interview, *Mobile Suit Gundam* ended its run with episode 43. Despite the shortened schedule and last-minute changes required, the show stuck its landing with a thrilling finale. Weary from their struggle, the animation team celebrated with a wrap party.

Dubbed the *Ceasefire Ceremony*, the party was held in House Suntory on the fifth floor of the Matsuoka Nishiogi Building, located by Nishi-Ogikubo Station in west Tokyo. This party formed the basis for the event seen earlier in the story, with Momoe moderating and Tomino leading the charge.

Even after the show went off the air, Tomino and the team continued relaying information to fans via anime magazines. There would be four *Gundam* movies, with a total runtime of ten hours! Even better, Yoshikazu Yasuhiko would return to redraw scenes from the show's latter half! This was the kind of thrilling info that readers found in the pages of the anime magazines of 1980—and the movie hadn't even been officially greenlit yet.

Even magazines with a less explicitly anime bent ran occasional features on *Mobile Suit Gundam*, with viewer opinions placed alongside information about the rebroadcast. Magazines also featured re-examinations of the TV version of the show, conversations with the team, and reviews of the novels. Some even had scoops on which parts of the country would be getting the rebroadcasts first.

Once the *Gundam* movie was greenlit, those sparks of fan enthusiasm roared into a blaze of glory, growing hotter and hotter in the leadup to the New Anime Century Declaration. But that's a story for another time... ◆

Animec #8

アニメックオリジナル対談、またまた登場!

「機動戦士　ガンダム」の最後はどうなるか?

総監督・富野喜幸

ガンダム終了決定!

なんと一月いっぱいで機動戦士ガンダムは終ってしまうのです。ガンダムの最後はどうなるのか? 数々の謎は解明されるのか? ファンにとっては気になることばかりです。再度、戦場のような制作現場をたずねて、総監督の富野喜幸氏にガンダムのお話をうかがいました。〈小牧〉

小牧　おじゃまします。ところでガンダムが3クールになったそうなんですが……(注・1クール＝13回)

富野　正確には3クールと1か月です。1月いっぱいまで放映ですね。決定が遅れたので最後を全部やり直さなくちゃいけないんです。あの雰囲気がガラッと変わって最後の10本ぐらいはかなりシビアになるでしょうね。

小牧　スケジュールがかなりきついのではないですか。

富野　いかんせん1月終了ってどれくらいかってことは、12月いっぱいで作画がほとんどおわらなきゃいけないのですが、全部ずれこんでいるから暮、正月はちょっと辛いですね。それに[illegible]らしく……過労なんですって。なにしろ人気者になってしまって……。

小牧　朝日ソノラマさんの、春からのクラッシャーのアニメ化はどうなりましたか?

富野　そんな話あるんですか?

小牧　うわさでは作監が安彦さんで演出は富野さんとかいう話で……。

富野　知らないですよ、そんな話。第一、今のサンライズがクラッシャー・ジョウをやるわけないですよ。

◇　◇　◇　◇　◇

小牧　今日は読者からの質問を持って来ているんです。テレビを見ていれば必然的に理解できるという事項は事典に入れたのですが、テレビから推察できない部分の説明をうかがいたいのですが……。

富野　それが一番困るんだよね。説明しきれないこともあるし……シャアのキズなんて解決してないですしね。

小牧　ポスターも見えるものと見えないものがありますからね。ガンダムフェスティバルのときの富野さんのお話[illegible]

富野　あたり前です。あるわけないんだもの。でも2話にあるなんてことはあの時言いませんでしたよ。ただ帳尻を合わせたいなあという話で……それさえ今はヤバくなって来てます(笑)。キズないんですよねェやっぱり……。

小牧　では。アムロの父テム・レイは生きているかも知れないという話を前にうかがったのですが、今後出て来ることありますか?

富野　まちがいなくテム・レイは登場します。アムロと再会して別れちゃいます。それはガンダムの話とは全然関係ないんです。本筋には関係ないかもしれませんが、アムロ自身の問題としては大変重要なことだと思える設き方になっています。この本が発売される頃、テム・レイが出て来ます。

小牧　これはもう言いまわしの問題だ[illegible]

▲Tomino went into detail on what was to come after the show went off the air.

Mobile Suit Gundam Complete Works, vol. 5

これが打上げパーティ企画書だ!

機動戦士
ガンダム
終戦協定調印式　招請状
（打上げパーティ）　御案内
＿＿＿＿様

N「宇宙世紀0079年。アニメに最もキビシイ宇宙植民地日本サンライズは、1スタ公国を名乗りアニメーション界にSFアニメ戦争を挑んできた。
この1ヵ年余りの闘いで、1スタ公国と外注軍は、総スタッフの半分を苦に至らしめた。スタッフは自らの行為に恐怖した。……
戦争は極限状態に陥り、1ヵ年余りが過ぎた。
この日、宇宙世紀0080年1月26日(土)長く厳しく苦しい戦いは終り、
君たちは、生き延びることができた!!
この戦いの後、サンライズ連邦政府と1スタ共和国の間で、終戦協定が結ばれる事になった。この協定調印式は下記の通りに行われる事になった。
生き延びた諸君は、この協定調印式を見届けるべく、こぞって参加される事を希望し、ここに心から招請状を発する次第であります。」

日時　1980年1月31日(木) PM. 6:30～9:30
場所　西荻窪 パブハウス サントリー館
西荻窪駅北口前 松岡西荻ビル 5F
機動戦士ガンダム最終回 ビデオ上映 テレビ4台のマルチ上映
8時～9時 ピアノ演奏あり、のど自慢の方は マイクがあります
すてきなウェイトレスが貴方のお相手です
すてきなウェイトレスの二人

☆いかにスタッフが、ガンダムを乗って製作していたかが判る好例がこの招請状だ。文章は、あの企画室の飯塚氏である。文章を読んで、楽しんでいただきたい。これがガンダムに関する最後の資料である。

Recent photo of the Matsuoka Nishiogi Building

◀▲The invitation to the wrap party, and the building where it was held. The building is still standing near Nishi-Ogikubo Station.

 Courtesy of: Sunrise, Masanobu Komaki, Matsuoka Jisho Co. Ltd.

1) Engineers drafted kit designs by hand at the time.
2) Wooden mold/prototyping manufacture.
3) Making finalized metal molds.
4) A row of molding machines.
5) Boxing the finished product.

In the years since, the release of a new *Gundam* series has always meant new Gunpla products for fans to enjoy in a variety of lines, from the beginner-focused High Grade line, to the more advanced Master Grade line. To date (2021), over 500 million models have been sold, and in 2011, Bandai began hosting the Gunpla Builders World Cup, allowing modelers from around the world to express themselves and compete using the universal language of Gunpla. ◆

Courtesy of: Bandai Co., Ltd.

Gunpla

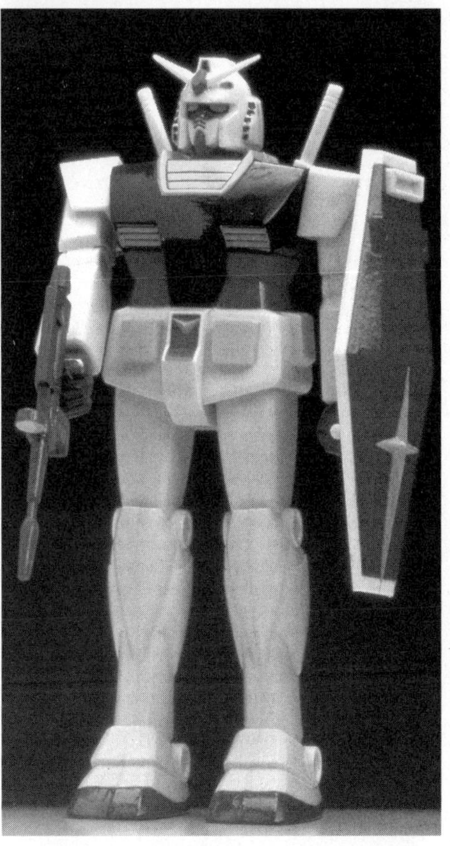

In July 1980, the year after *Mobile Suit Gundam* aired on TV, the 1/144 scale Gundam plastic model kit went on sale. It was the birth of Gunpla—**Gun**dam **pla**stic models.

In contrast to Clover, who produced a combining toy aimed at boys, the Bandai Hobby Department was able to parlay the success of their *Yamato* Best Mecha Collection series into a small-scale, low-cost line of *Gundam* models.

They also released a 1/100 scale version alongside the 1/144 kit, but unified scale on future releases. The result was a product that matched the fun of model building with the recognizability of character-driven merchandising. Model magazine features showcasing custom kits and specialized building techniques only fueled Gunpla's popularity, culminating in a Gunpla boom with the release of the third film.

The hobby department molding plant, originally located in Sodeshicho, Shimizu Ward, Shizuoka.

The current Bandai Hobby Center in Aoi Ward, Shizuoka.

THE MEN WHO CREATED
GUNDAM

EPISODE
14
RRMMMBBLL
A VOLCANO!
WHEN ONE ERUPTS, IT INDELIBLY ALTERS THE LIVES OF THOSE WHO LIVE IN ITS SHADOW!
ERUPTIONS ARE NOT FREAK OCCURRENCES, HOWEVER.
THERE ARE ALWAYS SIGNS.
ゴポ
BLRP
ゴポ
BLRP
AT THIS MOMENT, THAT VOLCANO WE CALL *GUNDAM* IS SHOWING SIGNS OF ACTIVITY.
G
AND WHEN IT BLOWS, THE WORLD WILL NEVER BE THE SAME AGAIN.

EPISODE
14
MOTOCOMPO
HONDA

LET'S SEE. THESE ARE KOGAWA'S KEYFRAMES,
AND THESE ARE ITANO'S, SO...
ふた
FWIP
あた
FWIP
UGH!! GUNDAM'S OVER, BUT WE'RE STILL SO BUSY!
CRRK
CRRK
MORNIN'.
OH, GOOD MORNING, SIR!
DON'T SUPPOSE YOUR TITS ARE SHOWIN ANY SIGNS O GROWTH?
むにゅ
GLMP
GRRP

WHOOPSIE-
DAISY!
SHWWIP

MWAHAHA!
YOU'LL
NEVER HIT ME
WITH AN
ATTACK LIKE
THAT!
OH.

WHAP
BONK
KASLAM
TWTCH
TWTCH
I FIGURED YOU'D DODGE IT, SO I HAD YOU JUMP TOWARD THE STAIRS.
YOU'RE IMPROVING BY THE DAY, KUSAKARI...

YEAH, BECAUSE YOU *NEVER LEARN!*
HMPH
HMPH
HAHA HA...

IF HIS DEBAUCHED DISRESPECT FOR PERSONAL SPACE IS IN PERFECT FORM, THEN SO IS THE MAN HIMSELF.
I WONDER IF HE'S GOT SOME GOOD NEWS TO SHARE.

Note: *Shonen Magazine* is Kodansha's flagship manga magazine for boys.

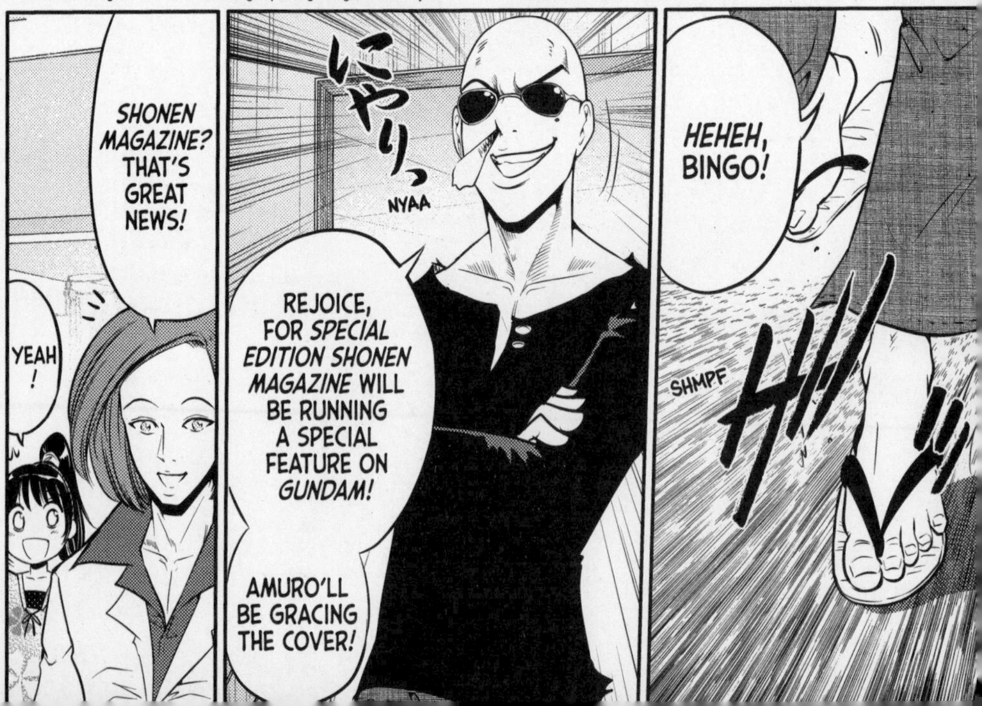

HEHEH, BINGO!
SHMPF
NYAA
REJOICE, FOR *SPECIAL EDITION SHONEN MAGAZINE* WILL BE RUNNING A SPECIAL FEATURE ON *GUNDAM!*
AMURO'LL BE GRACING THE COVER!
SHONEN MAGAZINE? THAT'S GREAT NEWS!
YEAH!

THE ANIME MAGAZINES WERE ALREADY COVERING *GUNDAM*.

BUT OTHER OUTLETS HAD YET TO COVER THE SHOW.

STARTING WITH *SPECIAL EDITION SHONEN MAGAZINE*, HOWEVER, THAT BEGAN TO CHANGE. MODEL MAGAZINE *HOBBY JAPAN*, FASHION MAGAZINE *POPEYE*,

AND SOON

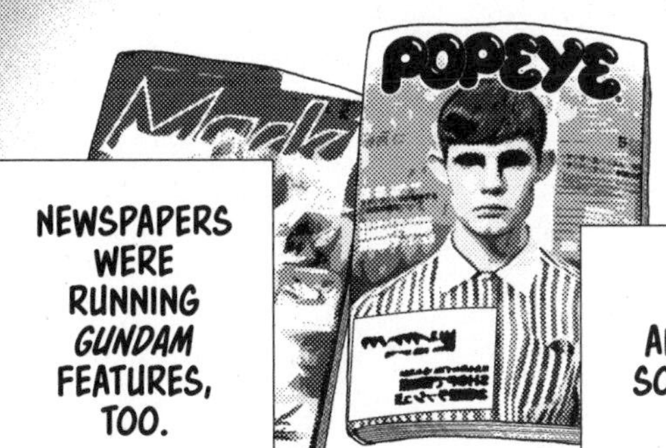

NEWSPAPERS WERE RUNNING *GUNDAM* FEATURES, TOO.

THE NEW JAPAN PHILHARMONIC EVEN RELEASED AN LP: *SYMPHONIC POEM GUNDAM*.

NORMALLY, THIS WOULD ALL HAPPEN BEFORE YOUR SHOW WENT OFF THE AIR!

THEN, IN THE SUMMER OF 1980

GUNDAM'S LOOMING WAVE GREW TOO LARGE TO IGNORE.

I SUPPOSE THERE'S NO IGNORING IT NOW.
FWPP
GUNDAM CLEARLY HAS A WAVE BEHIND IT.

OKAY, THEN. WE'LL DO IT.
WE'LL DISTRIBUTE GUNDAM FOR YOU.

HELL YEAH! GUNDAM'S GOING TO THE MOVIES, BABY!
COOL.
JUST LET US HANDLE THE BUSINESS DECISIONS.

WE'LL OPEN IN ROUGHLY THIRTY THEATERS,

ACROSS SATELLITE CITIES AND MAJOR METROPOLITAN AREAS.

JUST THIRTY?

IT'S A VERY REASONABLE NUMBER FROM A MARKETING STANDPOINT.

TH-THEN, HOW MANY THEATERS IS PART TWO GONNA OPEN IN?

PART TWO?!

THERE'S NOT GOING TO BE A PART TWO!

HA HA HA!

YOU GET ONE SHOT!

THAT'S ALL SHE WROTE!

I MIGHT RECONSIDER IN THE UNLIKELY EVENT YOU OUTDO *SPACE BATTLESHIP YAMATO.*

...

ARE YOU BEING STRAIGHT WITH ME RIGHT NOW?

HAHAHA. I SAID ***UNLIKELY.***

GO AHEAD AND UNDERLINE THAT PART.

SHOWA 55 · OCTOBER · 1980
S M T W T F S
1 2 3 4
5 6 7 8 9 10 11
12 13 14 15 16 17 18
19 20 21 22 23 24 25
26 27 28 29 30 31

I DIG THAT RESTAURANT YOU'VE GOT IN HERE—"ESCARGOT." MIND IF I BORROW IT ON OCTOBER 9TH?

THE ONE ON OUR TOP FLOOR? GO RIGHT AHEAD.

PLANNING TO THROW A LITTLE PARTY?

OH YES.

A PARTY.

MADE THE ZAKU THIS TIME, EH? AND CHAR'S, NO LESS!

LOOKIN' SHARP, LIL' GUY.
HEARING YOU SAY THAT MAKES ALL THOSE PAINFUL NIGHTS IN THE WORKSHOP WORTHWHILE.

THIS IS GONNA BE FLYIN' OFF THE SHELVES IN NO TIME!
...
WHAT'S UP?
NOTHING, IT'S JUST...

KYODA!
BAM
MR. PRESIDENT?!
ARE YOU MAKING JUNK IN HERE ON YOUR OWN AGAIN?!
SIR, THIS M.S. IS RIGHT BEHIND THE GUNDAM IN POPULARITY, SO—

I DON'T CARE! THE MEDIA LANDSCAPE'S CHANGING RIGHT BEFORE OUR EYES!
CHEAP TOYS BASED ON TV MANGA WILL NEVER SELL!

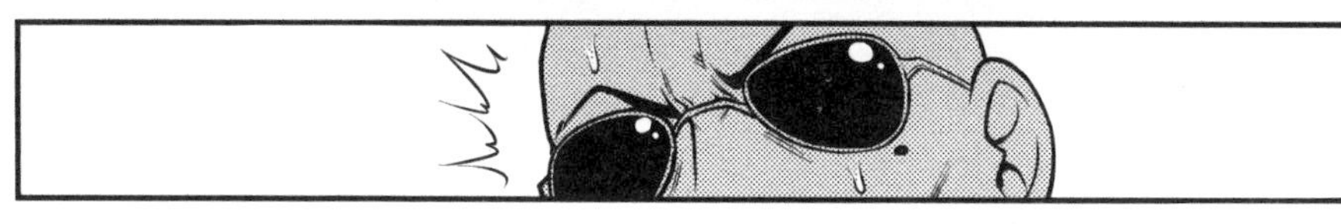

HMPH! IF YOU WENT TO THE TROUBLE OF MAKING A MOLD, YOU BETTER RECOUP THE COSTS! GOT IT?!
HAVE YOU SEEN THE MOUNTAIN OF LEFTOVER PRODUCT IN THE WAREHOUSE?!
THAT SPACE ISN'T FREE!
S-SIR!

JUST DO SOMETHING ABOUT THOSE PILES OF UNSOLD WHITE PLASTIC GARBAGE!
UNTIL THEN, I'LL BE WAITING FOR YOUR NECK!
バタン
SLAM
...
HAHAHA... CAT'S OUT OF THE BAG.
AS YOU CAN SEE, THE *GUNDAM* MODELS HAVE BEEN A TOTAL NON-STARTER, SALESWISE.
THEN WHY'D YOU MAKE THE ZAKU?

I GUESS YOU COULD SAY I'VE FALLEN IN LOVE. *HAH HAH!*

HANG ON JUST A LITTLE LONGER.

GUNDAM'S WAVE IS GETTING HUGE. IT'S GONNA REACH HERE TOO, GUARANTEED.

AND WHEN IT DOES, IT'S GONNA SEND THOSE MODELS FLYING OFF THE SHELVES.

YOU KNOW THE SAYING... "THE BIGGER THE WAIT, THE BIGGER THE WAVE."

HEH. NOT A BAD EXPRESSION.

WHO COINED IT?

I DID.

Note: Suguru Egawa was a pitcher for the Yomiuri Giants from 1979 to 1987.

GUNDAM SET TO BE NEXT YAMATO
Mobile Suit Gundam's protagonist, Amuron,
with young women.
THBOOOM
WHA-AAAT?!
BAM
R-R-RED ALERT, EVERYONE! THEY CONFIRMED THE GUNDAM MOVIE!
I-IT'S BEEN FORMALLY DECIDED?!

LOOK! OVER HERE, IN THE PAPER!
WHOA, SERI-OUSLY!

THEY'RE... ACTUALLY MAKING A MOVIE.
YEAH.
STILL CAN'T BELIEVE IT.
HEH. "AMURON." WHO WROTE THIS?

WELL...

THAT'S A WAVE, ALL RIGHT.

GUNDAM'S GETTING A MOVIE!
YES! YEEE-SSSS!
NEVER THOUGHT I'D LIVE TO SEE THE DAY!
YEAH!
OKAY, THEN.
SHP

WE'RE GONNA BE BUSY.

"IT WILL BE OPENING IN 150 THEATERS NATIONWIDE...

AS FOR FURTHER DETAILS...

A PRESS CONFERENCE WILL BE HELD OCTOBER 9 AT ESCARGOT, A RESTAURANT IN THE TOGEKI BUILDING..."

BAM

YOU'VE DONE IT NOW, KIDDO.

SOON ENOUGH, OCTOBER 9 ARRIVED.

EPISODE
15

Animec
EDITORIAL

HEY, KOMAKI.

THIS IS INOUE, OUR NEW PART-TIMER.

BOW

GLAD TO BE HERE.

PART-TIMER?

I'M AWFULLY BUSY. YOU DON'T NEED TO BRING EVERY RANDOM–

HM?

FWP

YOU'RE STUDYING AT WASEDA UNIVERSITY?
OH, WELL, YOU KNOW...

I BET YOU MUST BE GREAT WITH REPORTS!
ER, AH, SURE!
ZOOM
OKAY, THEN! EDITING FOR THE NEXT ISSUE'S ALL YOURS! OH DEAR, I'M EVER SO BUSY! TA-TA!
SHOOM
JUST LEAVE IT TO ME!
WAIT.
DOOOOOM
WHAAAAT?!

ER, W-WAIT!
SLAM
?!
WHAT SHOULD WE DO FOR THE *GUNDAM* FEATURE?
OH, AND ABOUT THOSE MERCH PAGES...
KOMAKI HAD PASSED THE BUCK WITH THE CAVALIER AIR OF AN IRRESPONSIBLE PARENT.
NY ORDINARY PART-TIMER WOULD HAVE HELPLESSLY WATCHED AS THE OFFICE DESCENDED INTO BEDLAM.
GRKK
BUT THIS WAS NO ORDINARY PART-TIMER.
THAT'S HOW IT'S GONNA BE, HUH?! FINE, I'M IN! LET'S GET THIS SHOW ON THE ROAD!
JUST ONE THING!
I TAKE NO RESPON-SIBILITY FOR WHAT'S ABOUT TO HAPPEN!

NONE COULD PREDICT IT, BUT IN TIME, HE WOULD BECOME PRESIDENT OF KADOKAWA SHOTEN.
INOUE'S SKILLS WOULD GROW BY LEAPS AND BOUNDS.
SHADDUP! I'M TAKING ALL THE REINS!
HUH? W-WE CAN'T CHANGE—
OKAY, WE'RE DOING A FEATURE ON *ANNE OF GREEN GABLES* NEXT!

Note: Kadokawa Shoten, now known simply as KADOKAWA, is the original publisher of this book and many Gundam books.

MRRMR
MRRMR
MRRMR
SORRY, ALMOST THERE!
HEY, QUIT PUSHIN'!
WHEN'S THIS THING STARTING?!
MRRMR
MRRMR
WHERE'S THAT STEPLADDER?!

Note: *Nikkan Sports* is a sports tabloid that's been in circulation in Japan since 1946.

Note: Pink Lady was a Japanese female pop duo that enjoyed a string of hits in Japan from 1976-1979.

THANK YOU FOR WAITING. WE'LL BE OPENING OUR DOORS SHORTLY.
AND WE'RE GOING TO SHOW THEM EXACTLY WHAT'S COMING NEXT.
OUTTA THE WAY! MOVE IT!
LOOK ALIVE, SHIT-HEADS!
RUSSSH
YOU GOT A GODDAMN DEATHWISH?!
MASS MEDIA FOLKS ARE PSYCHO, MAN.
そろ～…
SLLLNK
NO JOKE.
IT'S TIME WE HEAD INSIDE OURSE—
HM?

PKSH
PKASH
SNAP

SNAP
SNAP
PKASH
YOSHIYUKI TOMINO
PKSH

ムス
MMFF
ブスー
HUSHH
にこり
NYA

OH DEAR!
SUCH IMPOSING VISAGES ON THIS GRAND OCCASION!
HEY, TOMINO.
YEAH?

WHY DO I HAVE TO BE HERE?
I HATE THIS KIND OF THING.
WHAT CHOICE DO WE HAVE? YOU'RE THE ONLY GUY WE'VE GOT WITH ANYTHING RESEMBLING NAME RECOGNITION!

TOMINO, DO NOT, I REPEAT, DO NOT MENTION YOU-KNOW-WHAT.
YOU-KNOW-WHAT?

THE WHOLE TRILOGY BUSINESS!
I NEVER SIGNED OFF ON THAT!
WE'RE ANNOUNCING GUNDAM! NOT GUNDAM I. JUST GUNDAM!
AND I KEEP TELLING YOU, WE NEED MORE GODDAMN SCREENTIME!
SHH! IT'S STARTING!
JUST ANNOUNCE THE THING! NICE AND PROPER!
SNAP
...
PRODUCTION ANNOUNCEMENT
THANK YOU VERY MUCH FOR JOINING US HERE TODAY.
PKSH
SNAP
SNAP
PKSH
WITHOUT FURTHER ADO, WE WILL NOW BEGIN THE PRESS CONFERENCE ANNOUNCING THE MOBILE SUIT GUNDAM MOVIE.
PKSH

DUCTION
OUNCEMENT

DIRECTOR YOSHIYUKI TOMINO, IF YOU COULD OFFER A FEW WORDS?

HRMM

ER...

ANYTHING AT ALL, MR. TOMINO.

I GOT NOTHIN'.

TUNK
MRRMR
DON'T YOU DARE SASS ME!
HOW YOU LIKE THAT?
RRMMMBL
PKASH
PKSH
IF I HAVE TIME TO SAY ONE THING,
PKSH
IT WOULD BE TO EMPHASIZE THAT GUNDAM IS A TRUE GAME CHANGER FOR ANIME.
I'M YASUHIKO, ONE OF THE ANIMATORS.
PKSH
PKASH
FOR THE LOVE OF...
GRP

YOU'LL UNDERSTAND WHEN YOU SEE IT.

THIS IS WAY BEYOND *YAMATO*.

AN ANIME BEYOND...

ざわ MRRMR

ざわ MRRMR

YAMATO?

WELL PLAYED, YASUHIKO.

HM?

RIGHT. WELL, I THINK THAT SHOULD JUST ABOUT WRAP THINGS UP FOR TODAY.

I HATE THIS JOB.

HANDS TOGETHER, EVERYONE! SAY CHEE–

PRODUCTION ANNOUNCEMENT

GUNDAM

-SE!

PKASH

SO UH, THIS RED ROBOT IS GUNDAR?

ISN'T IT THAT TANK-LOOKIN' ONE?

ざわ
MRRMR

AMURON... AMURON...

ざわ
MRRMR

NOBODY SEEMS TO HAVE LEARNED ANYTHING FROM THE PRESS CONFERENCE.

DON'T WORRY, IT'LL BE FINE.

ガタ KLATTR
ガタ KLATTR
THE GOAL OF THE CONFERENCE WAS TO ALERT THE WORLD TO THE EXISTENCE OF SOMETHING "BEYOND *YAMATO*."
PEOPLE KNOW SOMETHING BIG'S GOING ON HERE. THAT'S WHAT MATTERS.
YOSHIYUKI TOMINO
ONCE THAT AWARENESS SPREADS, WE'RE GOING TO SEE ONE HECK OF A RESPONSE.
"WHAT'S THIS THING THAT'S BIGGER THAN *YAMATO?*" THEY'LL ASK.
THAT'S WHEN WE'LL ANSWER WITH OUR HEADS HELD HIGH,
"YOU'RE THINKING OF *GUNDAM!*"

KOMAKI...
NOW THEN. WE'VE GOT WORK TO DO!
スタスタ
TP
TP

THE RED ONE IS CALLED THE GUNCANNON.
THE TANK IS THE GUNTANK.
IF YOU'D LIKE TO SIT DOWN, I'D BE HAPPY TO EXPLAIN.
YOU'RE A LIFESAVER!
COUNT ME IN!

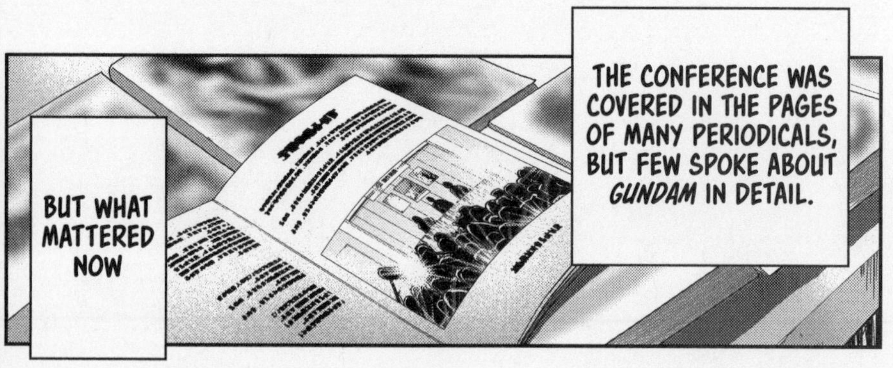

THE CONFERENCE WAS COVERED IN THE PAGES OF MANY PERIODICALS, BUT FEW SPOKE ABOUT *GUNDAM* IN DETAIL.
BUT WHAT MATTERED NOW

WAS THAT *GUNDAM* HAD TAKEN ITS FIRST BIG STEP TO THE SILVER SCREEN!

THE MEN WHO CREATED
GUNDAM

Confirming the *Gundam* Movie

THE PERIOD BETWEEN the end of *Gundam*'s TV broadcast in 1979 and the release of its film adaptation in 1981 was a banner year for anime movies. Besides the aforementioned *Be Forever Yamato*, audiences were dazzled by classics that are still discussed to this very day. The nightly TV listings, meanwhile, were home to new anime titles and reruns, night after night. Small wonder, then, that Shochiku finally agreed to make the *Gundam* movie a reality.

The Nikkan Sports article announcing the *Gundam* movie that Momoe Kusakari finds in the story describes a battle between Toei, Toho, and other major studios, with Shochiku wrenching the *Gundam* movie rights away from the industry's biggest names. When Yoshiyuki Tomino said that these were unheralded boom times for anime—and that the movie people would be tripping over themselves to secure the rights—he was right.

The article's headline describing *Gundam* as "the next *Yamato*," and the description therein of the battle between film studios for the opportunity to make the *Gundam* movie a reality, reveals the excitement and business expectations driving the industry in this era. ◆

Nikkan Sports, October 2, 1980

ポスト・ヤマトはガンダムだ

来春3月、松竹が1本立て公開

'81アニメ界殴り込み

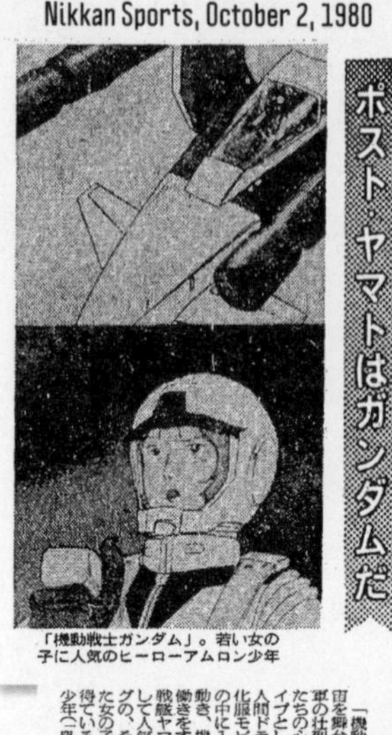

「機動戦士ガンダム」。若い女の子に人気のヒーローアムロン少年

ヤマトのつぎはガンダムだ！——大手映画会社が争奪戦を展開していたSFアニメ「機動戦士ガンダム」（日本サンライズ制作）が来年三月、春休みをねらって松竹で一本立て公開される。「ガンダム」は、昨年四月から今年一月にかけてテレビ朝日で放送されたが、最近になってが然人気が急上昇、アニメ雑誌の人気投票では「宇宙戦艦ヤマト」「銀河鉄道999」を抜いて断然トップに躍り出た人気アニメだ。これまでアニメに手を出さなかった松竹がこの「ガンダム」を武器に八一年アニメ界に殴り込むことになった。

□—□

「機動戦士ガンダム」は、宇宙を舞台にした連邦軍とジオン軍の壮烈な戦いを中心に、戦士たちの心のふれ合い、ニュータイプとしての目ざめなどを描く人間ドラマ。ガンダムは装甲強化服モビルスーツの名前で、この中に入った人間の意のままに動き、機能的には戦艦のような働きをする。これが巨大な宇宙戦艦ヤマトとは違った新兵器として人気を集めているが、ヤングの、それも十五歳を中心にした女の子の間で圧倒的な人気を得ているのはヒーローのアムロ少年(一四)と、敵方のシャア(一八)だ。

テレビ朝日で今年一月まで約一年間放送され、二〇％近い視聴率を挙げていたが、爆発的な人気となったのはここ二、三か月。「戦争を美化せず、現実的に表現し、キャラクターが人間くさくて血が通っている。放送が終わってから懐かしさが倍加した」＝加藤すえ子さん(一六)＝と、アニメ雑誌アニメージュ十月号の人気投票では一位にのし上がり、他の雑誌でも「ガンダム研究」特集が続々。

この異常人気に松竹、東映、東宝東和が劇場上映の名乗りを上げ、結局"アニメ処女"の松竹が上映権を手中に収めた。現在、二時間ものに再編集中。

来年は、東映が正月に大作「サイボーグ009超銀河伝説」三月に「白鳥の湖」八月に「銀河鉄道999Ⅱ」東宝が三月に「タブチくん3」など公開。アニメ・ラッシュの中で、果たして"ガンダム"がどこまで配収をのばすかみものだ。【谷口（過）】

▲ Photos of the nose section of the G-Parts and Sayla in her pilot suit were used in the article.

Courtesy of: Nikkan Sports

Announcing the *Gundam* Movie

Animec #15

Monthly OUT, December, 1980 Edition
▶ Tomino and Yasuhiko as they appeared at the press conference.

"ガンダム"映画化決定!!
来春3月、松竹配給で1本立公開

コメントが語られ、その後報道陣との質疑応答がなされた。各人のコメントの中で特に印象が深かったのがやはり富野さんの言葉で、「今まで俗悪番組の代表のように言われていたロボットアニメがこのような形で陽の目をみるようになったのは非常に嬉しい。"ガンダム"がこのように評価され多くのファンに受け入れられたのは、ロボットアニメでありながら人間関係を軸にした物語世界を築きあげていたからだと思う。スタッフを代表して感謝します」と映画化の喜びを語った。また安彦さんは、「"ガンダム"は自分にとって忘れられない作品だ。が、途中で病に倒れ製作現場から離れなければならなかったのが何とも心残りだ。しかしこの映画化を機会に、大きな画面にも耐えられる、またガンダムをそらんじている程に見ているファンにも十分楽しめ

◀ In an interview held a few days later, Tomino commented that "condensing 43 episodes into a single movie is physically impossible."

る作品に仕上げたい」と映画化への意欲を語った。
ファンの立場からしてみれば一番気になることは、劇場用の"ガンダム"がどのように再編集されるのか、とい

On October 9, 1980, at the Restaurant Escargot on the top floor of the Togeki Building in Tsukiji, the press conference announcing the *Gundam* movie was held, just as you saw in the story.

Present at the conference were Yoshiyuki Tomino and Yoshikazu Yasuhiko, as well as key personnel from Nippon Sunrise and Shochiku, who answered questions from members of the press following the announcement. The show had been cancelled a mere nine months prior, but it was finally happening. *Gundam* was getting a motion picture.

Yasuhiko expressed frustration over having to spend half the show's production schedule recuperating, while champing at the bit to wow audiences with the scale and power of the silver screen. Tomino, meanwhile, thanked the fans, but opted not to elaborate on the film's specifics. He instead hinted at the possibility of a movie series, stating that there was no way to compress the entire story into a single film, and that he didn't want to end it with just one entry.

Though the movie had been confirmed, Tomino and the team had to answer press questions while wondering whether they would get a chance to deliver the complete, serialized story they'd wanted to create from the beginning. ◆

Courtesy of: Masanobu Komaki, Asahi Paper Co., Ltd., Tetsuo Daitoku

THE MEN WHO CREATED
GUNDAM

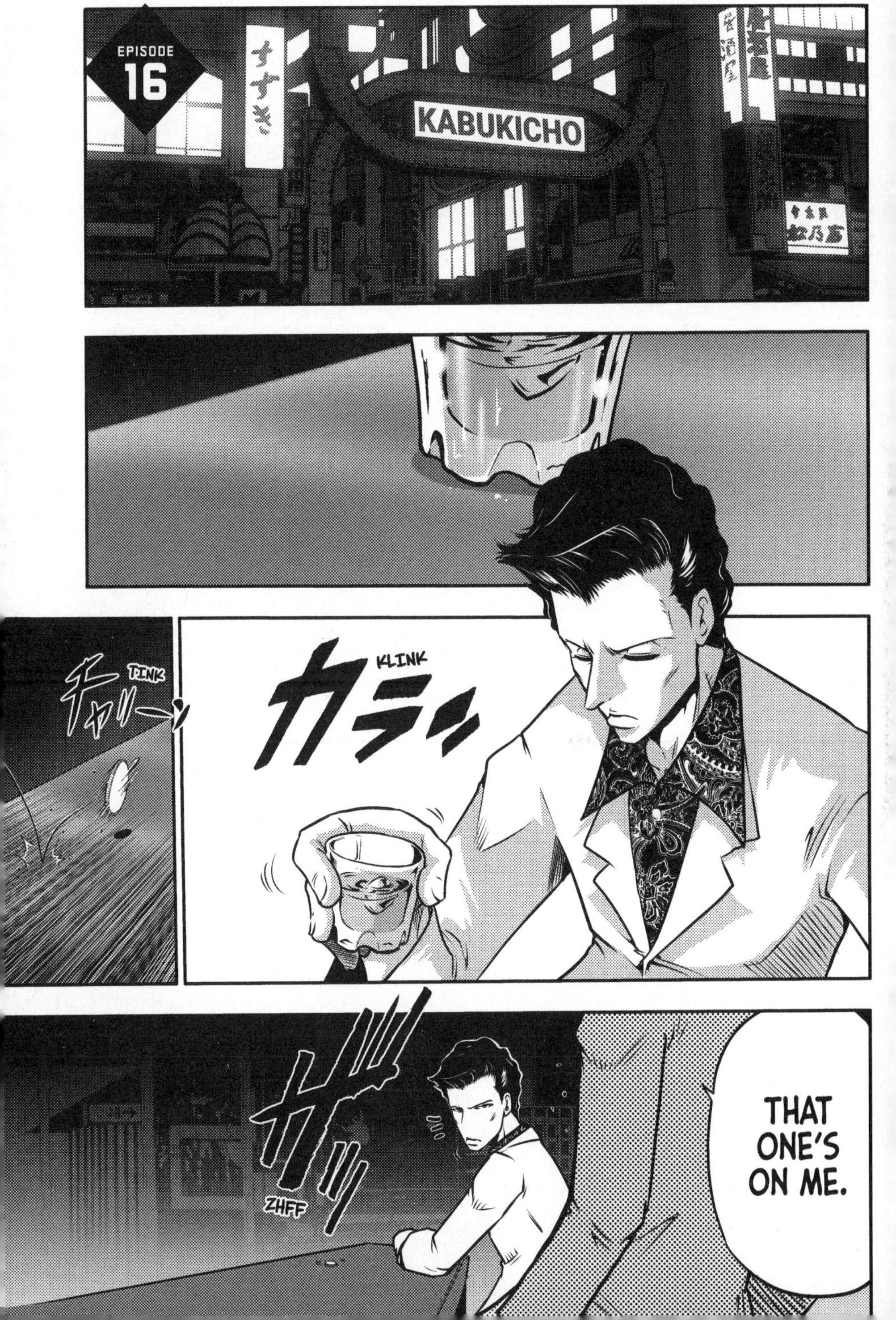

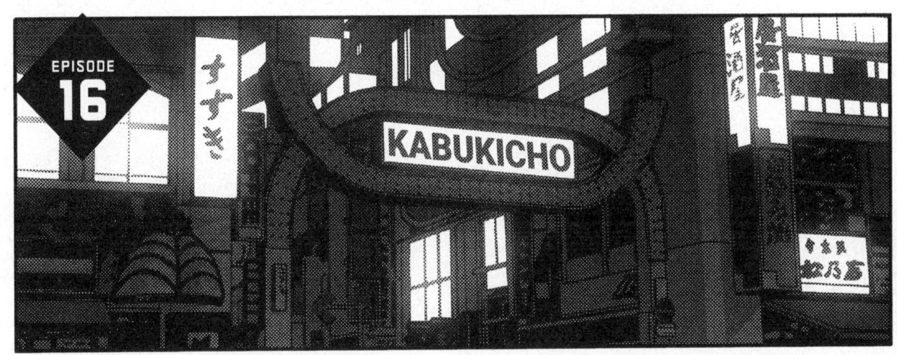
EPISODE
16
すすき
KABUKICHO

KLINK

TINK

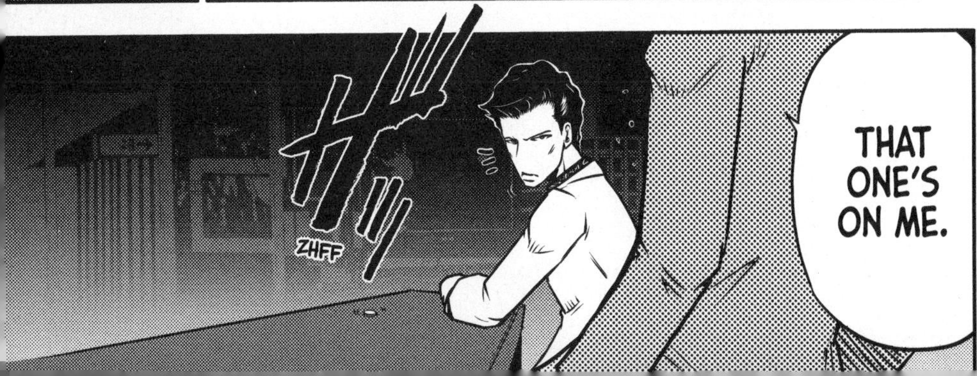
ZHFF
THAT ONE'S ON ME.

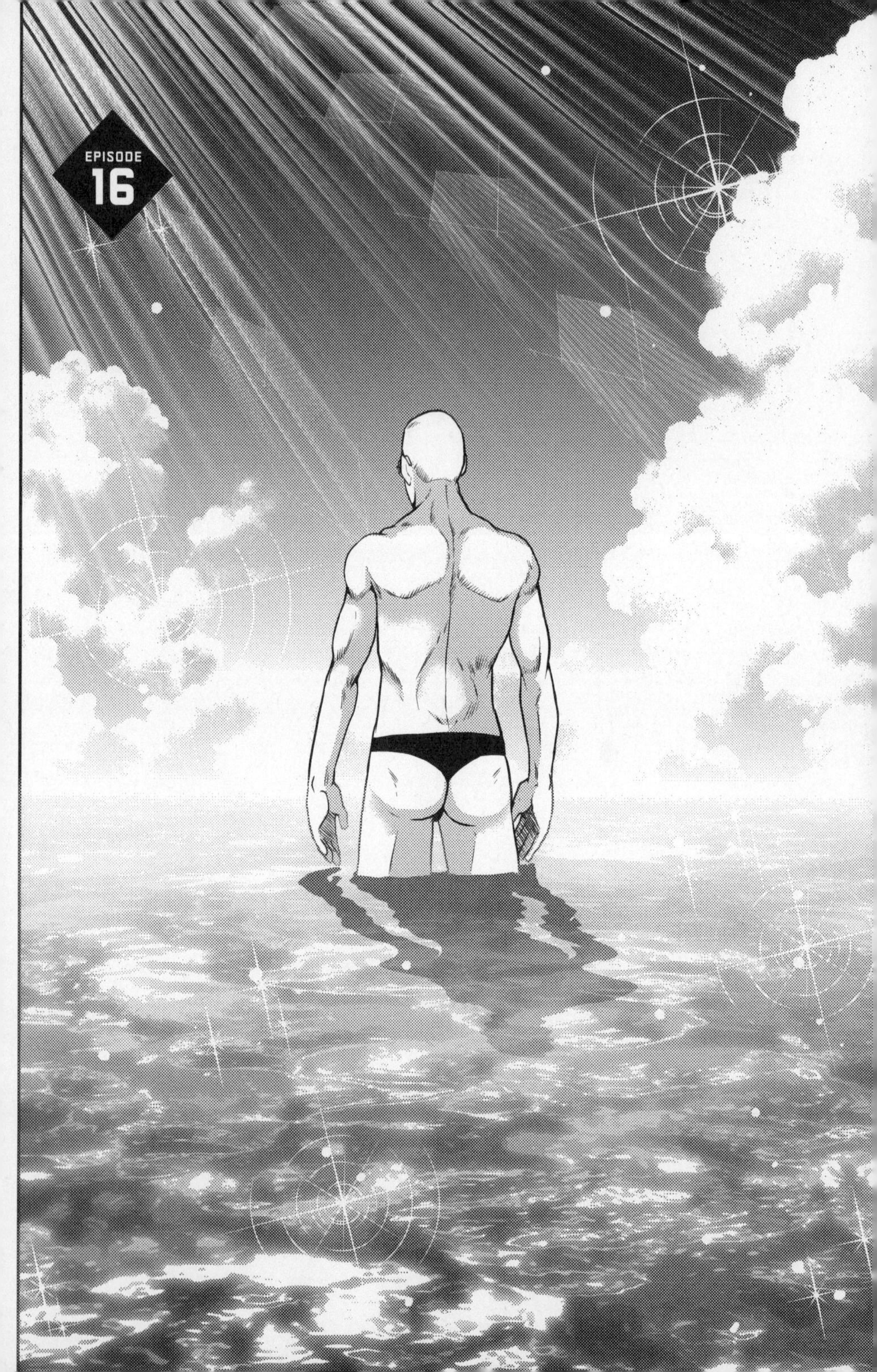
EPISODE
16

FROM SUNRISE, I TAKE IT?
HAHA, YOU COULD TELL?
WE'RE FROM SALES.
I CAN SMELL IT ON YOU.
NOBODY ELSE IN SHINJUKU WOULD TALK *GUNDAM*, THAT'S FOR SURE.
GUNDAM'S GETTING A MOVIE, MR. IKEDA!

IF IT DOES WELL, THERE MIGHT EVEN BE SEQUE—
GRRR
ER, IS EVERYTHING OKAY? YOU LOOK... UPSET.

KLNK
I WANT YOU TO TELL TOMINO SOMETHING FOR ME.

A MOVIE ISN'T SOME WALK IN THE PARK.
GOT IT?

RRMMMBL
S-SURE.
BY THIS POINT, SHUICHI IKEDA WAS ALREADY AN ESTABLISHED ACTOR.
HE'D SEEN TOO MANY PROJECTS EXPLODE ON THE RUNWAY TO REJOICE OVER A SIMPLE ANNOUNCEMENT.
HEH. I'M JUST PUTTING ON AIRS.
THANKS FOR COVERING MY TAB. TOODLES.
CRRK
UNDER-STOOD, SIR.
THE TOTAL COMES TO ¥150,000.*
SURE, ¥150—
GONG
WHAA-AAT?!
*Note: About $1,800 in 2021.

BOOOOM

MOTHER OF GOD, HOW MUCH DID HE DRINK?!

チュン
CHIRP
チュン
CHIRP

KAMI-IGUSA. KAMI-IGUSA.
SEIBU
プシュウー
FSHHHHH

プルルル
BRRRING
SEIBU RAILWAY
KAMI-IGUSA STATION

BRR, IT'S FREEZING!

SURE LOVE COMMUTING TO WORK ON A SUNDAY... HM?

I WONDER WHAT THEY'RE IN LINE FOR?
A NEW BAKERY, MAYBE?

ぞろぞろ
SHWOOM

WAIT. I KNOW THIS CORNER.

てくてく
TP TP

ドォオオオン
BDOOOOM

NIPPON SUNRISE

ざわざわ
MRRMR
MRRMR

THEY'RE IN LINE FOR US?! BUT WHY?!
RARR
RARR
RARR
RARR
YOU'RE LATE, KUSAKARI! GET YOUR ASS IN GEAR!
ONE AT A TIME, NOW...
WHAT ARE THEY WAITING IN LINE FOR, MR. YATATE?
CAN'T YOU TELL ?!
THEY'RE HERE FOR THE COMPLETE WORKS!

BAAAAM

THAT'S RIGHT! THE COMPLETE WORKS!

A SERIES OF OFFICIAL *GUNDAM* BOOKS PUT OUT BY SUNRISE THEMSELVES!

KOMAKI FROM *ANIMEC* HELPED EDIT THE BOOKS, LEADING TO THE INCLUSION OF NEVER-BEFORE-SEEN DESIGNS THAT TURNED THE SERIES INTO A TRUE MUST-HAVE FOR FANS.

THEY EARNED ACCLAIM AS FIRST-RATE ART BOOKS—A REPUTATION THAT REMAINS TO THIS DAY.

THEY WERE PRICEY, THOUGH. 2,900 YEN* PER VOLUME. AND BECAUSE THEY WERE MAIL-ORDER ONLY, YOU COULDN'T FIND THEM IN BOOKSTORES.

SOB

SOB

RGH...

ZASSH

THERE WERE EVEN THOSE WHO CLAIMED YOU WEREN'T A TRUE *GUNDAM* FAN WITHOUT THEM. TRULY THE STUFF OF LEGENDS.

* Note: About $43 in 2021.

YEAH, B-BUT WHY?!

RRMMBL

WE...

WE DIDN'T ACTUALLY PRINT THIS MANY COPIES... DID WE?

OKAY, PLAN B! GET THEIR NAMES AND ADDRESSES! WE'LL SEND THEM COPIES LATER!
GRAB A NOTEBOOK!
RUSSH
ON IT!
RRRRING
HELLO, YOU'VE REACHED NIPPON SUNRISE!
KLK
IS THAT YOU, KUSAKARI?
MR. KOMAKI?!
WE'RE GETTING FLOODED WITH CUSTOMER REQUESTS FOR THE COMPLETE WORKS!
I HAD A FEELING...
ANIMEC HAD A STORE IN SHINJUKU AT THE TIME, BENEATH THEIR OFFICE.
IT WAS A WELL-LOVED STOREFRONT THAT ALWAYS HAD GUNDAM GOODS ON OFFER.
HEY, NO PUSHING!
OW!
RARR

ANYWAY, I LET THEM KNOW TO HEAD TO YOUR NECK OF THE WOODS FOR COPIES.
HUH ?!
THE SEIBU LINE GOES STRAIGHT THERE FROM SHINJUKU, SO...
HM? THAT'S ODD.
ARE YOU LISTENING, KUSAKARI?
KUSA-KARI!
OH NO ...
RMMMBBLL
THERE'S EVEN MORE COMING ?!
THIS WAS NOT THE END.
IT WAS BUT A PRELUDE TO MUCH BIGGER THINGS TO COME.

EPISODE
17
THE SUN WAS RISING ON 1981.
THIS YEAR, *GUNDAM* WOULD ARRIVE ON THE BIG SCREEN AT LAST.
AH...
BWOOOSH
A FACT THAT HAS YOSHIYUKI TOMINO SHIVERING WITH JOY!
ACHOO!

EPISODE
17
ADDRESS YOSHIYUKI TOMINO
CURRENT ADD. BONITOBURG, SARDINEVILLE, CATNIP WARD, TOKYO
BORN 11/5/1941
ISSUED CARDBOARD BOX CENTRE, 123 CALICO TOWN, TAMA CITY, TOKYO
10/5/1981 2851
VALID UNTIL DEATH
CONDITIONS
RAY-NYANS FOR CAT EYES
TRY-X PUBLIC SAFETY COMMISSION
GREEN CAMEL
DRIVER'S LICENSE
LICENSE NUMBER
1234567890 YOSHIYUKI TOMINO
LICENSE DATES
ISSUE DATES
MC
OTHER
TYPE 2
10/5/1981 3
0/0/0000 0
0/0/0000 3
VALIDITY
0 1 0 1 0 1 0 1 0 0 0
LICENSE CATEGORY
ROLLER COASTER
TRICYCLE
STILTS
MOTOR-CYCLE
HELICOPTER
MOPED
RICKSHAW
BICYCLE
YAMATO
APOLLO
BULLET TRAIN

ジャラ…
SHLUMP

AW, SHUCKS. I'M BROKE.
MY DAYS OF SUPPORTING *GUNDAM* MONETARILY MAY BE NUMBERED.

OH, I KNOW!
THE NEW M.P. ZAKU KIT SHOULD BE OUT BY NOW!
IF IT'S 1/144 SCALE, I CAN PROBABLY–
BWUH?

Tanaka Toys
TOYS
ざわ
MRRMR
ざわ
MRRMR
ざわ
MRRMR
WH- WHAT THE?
カラ
KLNK
GIMME THE GUNDAM!
ざわ
MRRMR
ざわ
MRRMR
I DON'T WANT A DUMB MUSAI!
HOW ABOUT Z'GOKS?
YA GOT Z'GOKS?!

U-UM...

HEY! GUNDAM GUY!

WHAT'S GOING ON HERE?!

THE HECK IS THIS *GUNDAM* THING, ANYWAY?!

RARR

RARR

IT'S HAPPENING...

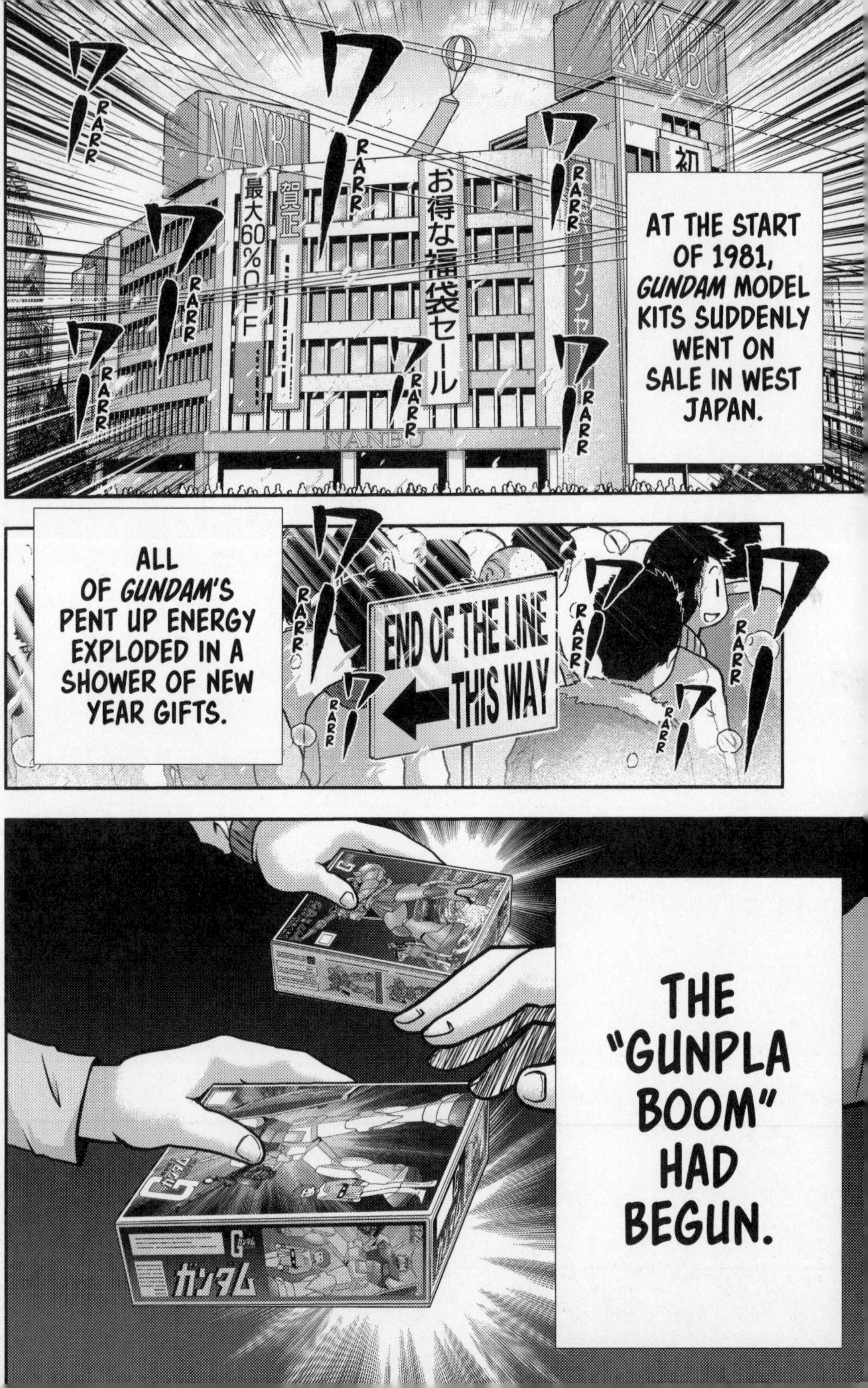

ALL OF *GUNDAM'S* PENT UP ENERGY EXPLODED IN A SHOWER OF NEW YEAR GIFTS.

THE "GUNPLA BOOM" HAD BEGUN.

SEIBU RAILWAY
KAMI-IGUSA STATION

WOW...
THESE SUNDAY MORNING LINES ARE A WEEKLY THING NOW, HUH?
RARR RARR RARR RARR

SO MUCH FOR MY SUNDAY PLANS...
GOOD PROBLEM TO HAVE, THOUGH. RIGHT?

GRRRRR
PFT

EEP! WH- WHAT'S GOING ON?!
THAT WAS MURDER IN YOUR EYES!
DON'T SAY SHIT LIKE THAT!
IDEON'S BEEN CANCELLED.
HUH?
OH...
THAT EXPLAINS IT.
TCH...
SPACE RUNAWAY IDEON.
YOSHIYUKI TOMINO'S DARING FOLLOW-UP TO GUNDAM. (ITS TV RUN STARTED IN 1980.)

ファサ…
FWSSH
A HARD SCI-FI STORY WITH REALISTIC CHARACTERS. NOT MONSTER-OF-THE-WEEK FARE.
IT HAD ALL THE ELEMENTS THAT MADE *GUNDAM* A HIT...

INCLUDING THE PART WHERE IT ***GOT CANCELLED,*** AM I RIGHT?
HAHAHA!
BWAHA-HAHA!

IDEON, HUH.
HOW'D YOU CONVINCE A SPONSOR TO PAY FOR A SHOW THAT DARK?

I DIDN'T.
HUH?
IT WOULD NEVER MAKE IT PAST 'EM.
FSHWAAAAH
WAIT, DOES THAT MEAN...
RMBLL
OHHH NO!
AOYAGI
ALL RIGHT, TIME FOR THE NEXT PROJECT.
RIGHT.
GUNDAM ALMOST SANK THE COMPANY.
I'M BEGGING YOU. KEEP IT SIMPLE THIS TIME!

GOT IT. ...HM?
GANDROWA (TBD)
WHAT'S THE DEAL WITH THIS PROJECT?
IT'S FROM ONE OF OUR TOY COMPANY SPONSORS.
GOTTA MOVE THOSE TOYS.
I'LL HANDLE THIS ONE.
YOU KNOW WHAT THEY SAY. THE SHOW MUST GO ON.
RTTL
WHOA, NEVER THOUGHT I'D HEAR THAT FROM YOU! SURE, IT'S ALL YOURS.
NOW, IF YOU'LL TAKE A LOOK AT THE PRINTOUTS I GAVE YOU...
RUNAWAY

MECHA A
MECHA A IS AN ARMORED VEHICLE.
IT'S PILOTED BY THE PROTAG-ONIST, COSMO YUKI.
PASSENGER DOOR
TREADS
RETRACTS
HERE'S MECHA B.
IT'S A TANKER TRUCK. KIDS LOVE THESE THINGS.
MECHA B
DOOR
MECHA C
AND HERE'S MECHA C. A BUS.
ASHURA AND PIPER LOU TAKE IT TO KINDERGARTEN.

IDEON
MECHA A
THE THREE MECHA COMBINE INTO IDEON, A TOWERING ROBOT.
THIS WILL BE A FUN ACTION SHOW ABOUT PROTECTING THE WORLD—AND YOUR NEIGHBOR-HOOD.
THOK
OOH, THAT SOUNDS FUN!
SURE DOES! WHAT KID DOESN'T LOVE A COMBINING ROBOT?
I CAN'T WAIT TO SEE IT.
IT'S IN GOOD HANDS.
BAM
OKAY.
HAVE THE TOY GUYS LEFT THE BUILDING?
YEAH, IT'S JUST US NOW.

THROW OUT ALL THE SHIT I JUST SHOWED YOU.
I'M GONNA TELL YOU WHAT'S REALLY GOING ON.
ER, SIR?
THESE ARE THE RUINS OF THE SIXTH CIVILIZA-TION.

WHEN I SAW THIS ROBOT, I KNEW...
NYAA
THIS IS IDE, MY FRIENDS!

BWAA-AAA-AH?
UH, SIR?
WHAT ARE YOU TALKING ABOUT?

DON'T MOUTH OFF TO ME! I'M TALKIN' RUINS HERE!
SMASH
WAAUGH! FORGIVE ME!
NIPPON SUNRISE
AS
OR WHAT
APPENED
NEXT...

SPACE RUNAWAY IDEON BECAME A SHOW ABOUT HUMANS WAGING MERCILESS WAR AGAINST EACH OTHER.
IT ENDS WITH BOTH SIDES BEING WIPED OUT. DEFINITELY *NOT* A SHOW FOR KIDS!
THE TOYS SAT ON THE SHELVES, AND THE SHOW WAS CANCELLED IGNOMINIOUSLY.

SO, YOU SCAMMED THEM?
HOW MANY TIMES HAVE YOU TRICKED SPONSORS LIKE THIS?
GOSH, YOU'RE DENSE! IF YOU CAN'T FOOL A SPONSOR, YOU'RE *NEVER* FOOLIN' THE AUDIENCE!

K-KILL 'EM ALL TOMINO...

THANKS TO *GUNDAM*, *IDEON* WOULD LATER ENJOY A REVIVAL, BECOMING A LEGEND IN ITS OWN RIGHT.

BUT THAT'S A STORY FOR ANOTHER TIME.

EPISODE
18
PAPICON

ざわ
MRRMR
ざわ
MRRMR

GOODNESS, THIS IS QUITE THE TURNOUT FOR NEW YEAR'S!

ISN'T IT, THOUGH? I HAVEN'T SEEN LINES LIKE THESE SINCE *THE ELEPHANT MAN*!

HM?

スタ
SHFFL
スタ
SHFFL
ODD. IS IT ME, OR ARE THE PEOPLE IN LINE GOING HOME WITHOUT WATCHING ANYTHING?

RAHH
YOU'RE RIGHT. THEY'RE ALL YOUNGSTERS, TOO.
RAHH

HEY, HOW'S ATTENDANCE FOR THE DAY LOOKING?
OH, ABOUT THE USUAL, I'D SAY.
NOTHING OUT OF THE ORDINARY.

RMMMBLLL

ATTENDANCE IS... NORMAL?

WITH THOSE LINES?

THEY'RE FOR ADVANCE TICKETS.

ADVANCE TICKETS?
THEY'RE WAITING IN LINE JUST TO BUY A TICKET FOR A MOVIE LATER?
ざわ
MRRMR
ざわ
MRRMR
WHAT KIND OF MOVIE DOES THAT?!
GUNDAM SOLD 100,000 ADVANCE TICKETS?!
AND IT DID IT IN A WEEK?!

YESSIR. AND THEY KEEP SELLING. WE'RE ADDING SAME-DAY TICKETS, TOO.

RGH...

FATH— ER, SIR, DOES THIS MEAN...

RRRRING
NIPPON SUNRISE
CHK
YELLO? WHY, IF IT ISN'T MR. PRESIDENT!
HONESTLY, I FIGURED I'D BE GETTING A CALL FROM YOU.

SO,
WE GET OUR ANSWER?
...
HEH.

YOU WIN THIS ONE, TOMINO.
WE LOSE.

NYAA
にやり
IN OTHER WORDS...

GUNDAM II WAS GETTING MADE!
AND SO WAS III! THE GUNDAM MOVIES WERE OFFICIALLY A TRILOGY!
BDOOOOM
YESSS!
NIPPON SUNRISE

WELL, I'M GLAD IT'S OFFICIAL!
GRP
YEAH, LAYING THE GROUND-WORK WITHOUT KNOWING FOR SURE WAS ROUGH!
SO WHEN'S *II* OPENING?
THIS SUMMER.
SUMMER HUH. GIVING US A RELEASE WINDOW ON SUMMER VACATION, HM?
SSSSP
GREAT, THAT SHOULD GIVE KIDS A CHANCE TO—
WAIT.
THIS SUMMER ?!
SPPPSSHHH
IT BURNS!

PART ONE OPENS THIS SPRING! ARE YOU DENSE?!
III OPENS NEXT SPRING.
FORGET DENSE! YOU'RE INSANE!
GRRRAAH
NEXT... SPRING? DOES THAT MEAN...
WE HAVE TO MAKE THREE MOVIES IN A YEAR?!
GONG
AND QUIT YOUR COMPLAINING. THE TV SERIES GIVES US PLENTY TO WORK WITH.
JUST GOTTA ADD A CHERRY OR TWO ON TOP.
SNIP
WAAH!
SPARE ME THE WATER-WORKS!

I'LL EDIT THIS THING TOGETHER MYSELF.

YOU WILL?
MRRMR
OH, *TOMINO'S* GONNA EDIT IT!
NOW I GET IT. WE *CAN* DO THIS!

WHAT DO YOU MEAN?
AH, YES. THIS WAS BEFORE YOU JOINED, KUSAKARI.

TOMINO'S A GENIUS IN THE EDITING ROOM.

BY THE END OF *ZAMBOT 3*, THE TEAM WAS SCRAMBLING TO MEET DEADLINES.

WE WERE CONVINCED WE WOULDN'T MAKE IT.

THAT'S WHEN HE STEPPED INTO ACTION.

RAAR

RAAR

RAAR

RAAR

SNIP

HE STRUNG THE ODDS AND ENDS THEY'D COBBLED TOGETHER INTO A FINISHED EPISODE!

EPISODE 20, "BEFORE THE FINAL BATTLE," TO BE EXACT!

HE WORKED SIMILAR MAGIC ON *DAITARN 3*'S "MEGABORG MADNESS,"
SEAMLESSLY WEAVING PATCHWORK ELEMENTS TOGETHER.
IT EARNED HIM A NICKNAME ...

"TOMINO THE WEAVER."
I'VE HEARD THE NAME BEFORE.
A SKILL I LEARNED WHEN I WAS JUST STARTING OUT. WHEN I HAD TO ACCEPT INSANE SCHEDULES TO SURVIVE.
NOTHING WORTH PUTTING ON A PEDESTAL.

MAKING THREE MOVIES IN A YEAR?
IT'S ENOUGH TO MAKE ME VOMIT IN TERROR.
THAT SAID...
THERE'S *ONE THING* WE HAVE TO FIX.

HAD A FEELING THIS WAS COMING.
IMPLEMENTING A FIX IS GONNA TAKE SOME SERIOUS DOING.
THERE'S NO REASON TO REMAKE THIS THING, OTHERWISE.
WE FIX IT, OR I'M OUT.
RMMMBL
C'MON, DIRECTOR.
GIVE ME *SOME* CREDIT.
KRRK
YOUR REQUEST'S ALREADY DONE.
HUH?
SHF

CORE BOOSTER
BKOOOOM
SHIING
THE CORE BOOSTER.
SAYLA PILOTS IT INSTEAD OF THE G-FIGHTER.

RGH!
WHEN DID YOU PUT IN THE REQUEST FOR THIS?
"MOVIES DON'T NEED TOYS."
AIN'T THAT RIGHT?

...
HMPH. IF THE G-FIGHTER'S GETTING REPLACED, *II*'S GOING TO NEED A REHAUL FOR THE SUMMER.

I COULD CLONE MYSELF, AND WE WOULDN'T HAVE ENOUGH MANPOWER.

Note: The "Last Shooting" refers to a scene from *Gundam III*, in which the Gundam stretches its right arm for a final beam cannon shot.

THE ONE YEAR WAR—

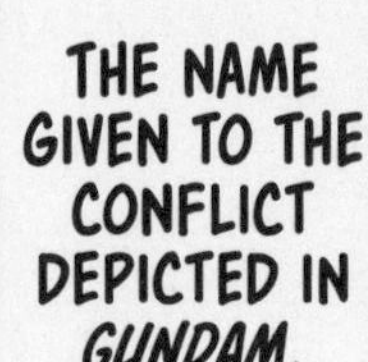
THE NAME GIVEN TO THE CONFLICT DEPICTED IN *GUNDAM*.

MUCH LIKE THE CREW OF THE WHITE BASE, *GUNDAM'S* PRODUCTION TEAM FOUGHT LONG AND HARD OVER THE COURSE OF A YEAR.
SKF

THIS WOULD BE *GUNDAM'S* FINAL YEAR.

THE ONE YEAR WAR HAD BEGUN.

THE MEN WHO CREATED
GUNDAM

Mobile Suit Gundam Complete Works

Mobile Suit Gundam Complete Works, vol. 1

An ad in *Animec* #15 for the *Complete Scripts* and *Complete Works*.

▲ Due to the unique way in which it was sold, the ad prominently featured detailed purchase instructions.

Mobile Suit Gundam Complete Works was a five-volume series of official data books released by Sunrise. After the release of the fifth volume, a script collection entitled *Mobile Suit Gundam Complete Scripts* was released between December 1980 to December 1981.

Each *Complete Works* volume included a story digest, detailed character and Mobile Suit bios, along with staff interviews and stories from inside Sunrise. Articles detailing the early stages of production were also included, giving readers a sense of the surrounding context behind the show's creation. *Animec* E.I.C. Masanobu Komaki contributed to the book as well. When he describes the *Complete Works* as first-rate, he's only speaking the truth.

The fifth volume of *Complete Works* also included legendary Tomino Memo segments, elaborating on how the series would have *really* ended if it hadn't been cancelled.◆

Courtesy of: Sunrise, Masanobu Komaki

Advance Tickets

Ticket stubs for the *Mobile Suit Gundam* films.

▲ The ticket stubs prominently featured the main visuals from the films. The prices are a time warp back to the '80s, too.

THE ADVANCE TICKETS for the *Gundam* movie trilogy give us a hint to its shocking box office performance. As portrayed earlier in the story, strong advance ticket sales for the first film were key to ensuring the *Gundam* movie became a trilogy.

Fans lined up to purchase advance tickets for *II* and *III*, giving them a sense of participation and celebration that would link directly into the New Anime Century Declaration later on. Every time advance tickets for the next entry in the trilogy went on sale, movie theater attendants cocked their heads in bewilderment as fans lined up, bought their tickets, and went home without watching anything.

When the release of *Encounters in Space* drew near, theaters deployed the film's imagery and posters on front-facing standees to help drive advance ticket sales, and fans would excitedly gather around them throughout the night as they waited for the big day. The pamphlet for *Encounter in Space* includes a mention of the late-night lines, which became a true barometer of *Gundam*'s burgeoning popularity. ◆

THE MEN WHO CREATED
GUNDAM

MOBILE SUIT GUNDAM DREW MANY TALENTED CREATORS WITH ITS PROMISE OF REVOLUTION.
YOSHIYUKI TOMINO, YOSHIKAZU YASUHIKO, AND KUNIO OKAWARA WERE ONLY THE TIP OF THE ICEBERG.
IN GUNDAM'S RADIANCE, COUNTLESS NEW TALENTS SPRANG INTO BLOOM.
EPISODE 19
1979— IN A CERTAIN STUDIO IN TOKYO.
HEY!
SHINANO PRO
BAM
WHO'S RESPONSIBLE FOR THESE IN-BETWEENS?
TODAY'S THE DEADLINE FOR HAWK OF THE GRAN PRIX!
SHF
FWSH
THAT WAS ME.
THIS MAN WAS ONE OF THOSE TALENTS.

ICHIRO ITANO.
ゆら
WOBBL
THE ANIMATOR WHO WOULD GO ON TO STUN THE WORLD WITH THE "ITANO CIRCUS."
EPISODE 19

WAS THERE A PROBLEM WITH MY IN-BETWEENS?

YOU AGAIN?!
LISTEN. THE SCENE'S SIMPLE. THE KEY FALLS, IT HITS THE GROUND. DONE!

JUST SPACE IT OUT, START TO END!
SHP
ADD ONE MORE MOVEMENT, AND YOU'RE DONE!
WHAT PLANET ARE WE TALKING ABOUT HERE?
'SCUSE ME?

WE DERIVE MOVEMENT FOR A FALLING BODY WITH $d = \frac{1}{2}gt^2$

ONE FRAME IS 1/24THS OF A SECOND, SO 0.04167, WHICH GETS US t.

さらさら

SKRCH

UH...

WE USE TWO IN-BETWEEN FRAMES TO CAPTURE THE MOVEMENT.

GRP

WE USE THE REMAINING FRAME FOR THE KEY'S REBOUND.

THE RESULT: CONSIDERABLY GREATER REALISM.

FIVE FRAMES TOTAL. NO DIFFERENCE IN COST.

WHAT WAS THE ISSUE AGAIN?

JUST FILLING IN THE GAPS BETWEEN THE KEY FRAMES IS ENOUGH.

CAN'T MAKE A LIVING OTHERWISE WITH IN-BETWEENS PAYING PEANUTS.

SO QUIT OBSESSING OVER EVERY POINTLESS LITTLE FRAME!

ICHIRO ITANO WAS STARTING TO QUESTION THE INDUSTRY'S AGE-OLD WAYS OF DOING THINGS.

"WHY TURN AWAY FROM REALITY?" HE WONDERED.

AT THE TIME, NOBODY ELSE WAS FOCUSING ON THE SIMPLE MOVEMENT OF OBJECTS.

Café Pop
☎ 983-8990

A NEW ANIME SERIES?

YEAH, THE PLACE I'M AT NOW IS WORKING ON IT, AND IT'S SOMETHING ELSE.
IT'S ABOUT A WAR BETWEEN HUMANS, FOR ONE THING.

THE ROBOTS AREN'T SUPER-HEROES. THEY'RE WEAPONS.
SSSIP
THE SHOW'S STRIVING TO BE MORE THAN A MERE TOY COMMERCIAL.
...

HAMATSU.

COULD YOU TELL ME A LITTLE MORE ABOUT THIS THING?

NIPPON SU
ITANO KNOCKED ON NIPPON SUNRISE'S DOOR THE NEXT DAY. GOOD EYE, YOU MIGHT SAY.

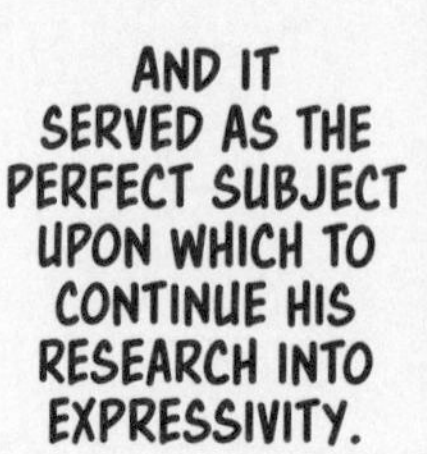
AND IT SERVED AS THE PERFECT SUBJECT UPON WHICH TO CONTINUE HIS RESEARCH INTO EXPRESSIVITY.

企 画 日本サンライズ
GUNDAM WAS CLEARLY UNLIKE ANY ANIME THAT HAD COME BEFORE.

HE BECAME SO ABSORBED IN THE WORK, HE FORGOT TO EAT AND SLEEP.

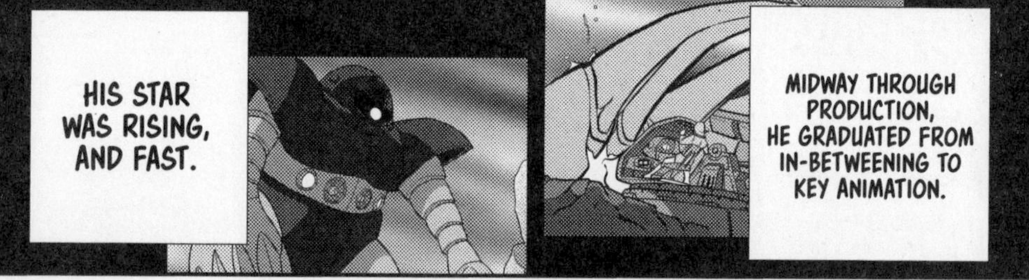
HIS STAR WAS RISING, AND FAST.
MIDWAY THROUGH PRODUCTION, HE GRADUATED FROM IN-BETWEENING TO KEY ANIMATION.

THEN, ONE DAY ...
UGH ...
OOGH ...

SOB...

DIRECTOR TOMINO?

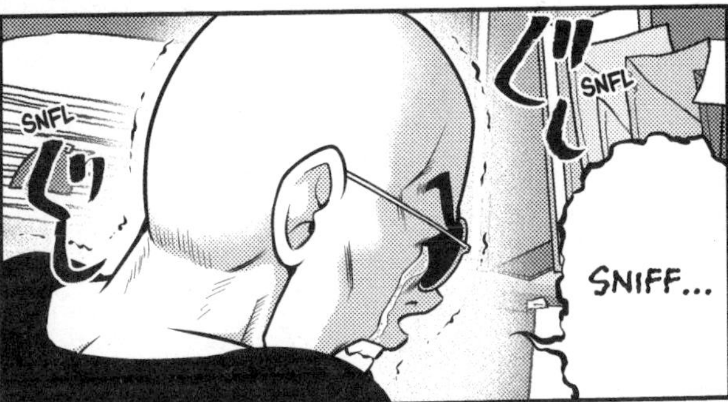

BAMMM
HE'S CRYING OVER HIS OWN STORYBOARD?!

STORY-BOARD'S DONE, YASUHIKO! CHECK IT OUT!
FWOM
UH, SURE?

WHAT'S WITH THE CRYING? GET YOUR ACT TOGETHER, MAN.

KRREE
LET'S TAKE A LOOK.

FLP

ペラ
FLP
ペラ
FLP
…
ペラ
FLP
?
KWIVR
プル
プル
ダー
SOOOB

ZZ
THIS IS REALLY GOOD, TOMINO!
FWMP
AIN'T IT, THOUGH?
YASUHIKO TOO?!

#28 ACROSS THE ATLANTIC
EPISODE 28. SPY GIRL FOLLOW-UP?
MUST BE ONE HELL OF A STORY-BOARD.
OKAY, LET'S START THE STORYBOARD MEETING.
YEAH!
WHOO HOO

THERE,

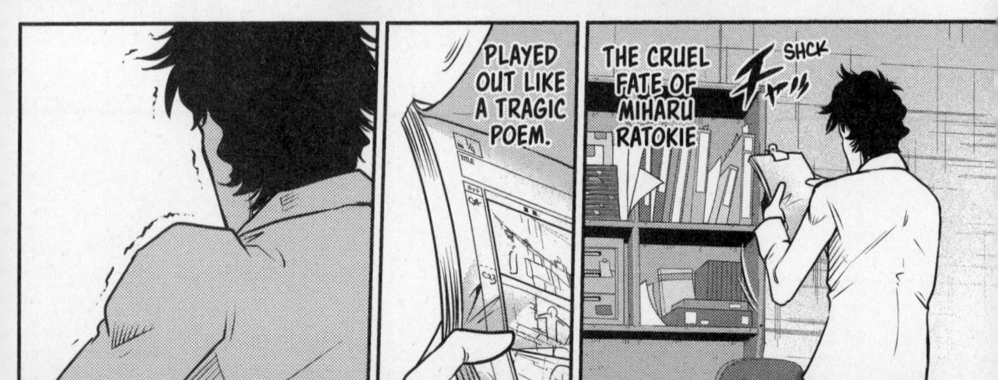

THE CRUEL FATE OF MIHARU RATOKIE
SHCK
PLAYED OUT LIKE A TRAGIC POEM.

BWAH
#28
Across the Atlantic

NIPPON SUNRISE
EPISODE 31, "A DECOY IN SPACE," IS UP NEXT. WE'RE FINALLY GOING BACK TO THE STARS.
IT'S THE START OF A NEW CHAPTER.
AND WITH IT, THE STORY'S CLIMAX.
BWOOOSH
WE'VE GOTTA DO SOMETHING MEMORABLE FOR THE WHITE BASE'S DEPARTURE FROM JABURO!
LIKE HAVIN' A THOUSAND FLAMINGOS FLAPPIN' UP INTO THE SKY!
A THOUSAND FLAMINGOS? OH GOD...
ざわ
MRRMR
DO **NOT** SIGN ME UP FOR THAT.
COME ON. NOBODY WANTS TO TACKLE IT?
I'LL DO IT.

HARD TO PUT INTO WORDS, BUT I'VE MADE A VOW TO MYSELF.

A VOW TO PUT ABSOLUTELY EVERYTHING I HAVE INTO THIS PROJECT.

ITANO...

GRIN

THE DEPARTURE FROM JABURO BECAME A LEGENDARY SCENE, WITH THE WHITE BASE, FLAMINGOS, AND SETTING SUN CREATING A TRULY GORGEOUS CONTRAST.

THE FLAPPING WINGS OF EVERY FLAMINGO ANIMATED IN PAINSTAKING DETAIL.

A LEVEL OF DETAIL BORDERING ON THE DIVINE.

DASSSHH

BAM
Y-YOU'RE NOT GONNA BELIEVE THIS!
WHAT HAP-PENED?

YASUHIKO, H-H–
HUFF HUFF

HE COLLAPSED!
BAAAAM
HUH?!
GUNDAM'S CREATORS NOW FACED THE THREAT OF ABJECT RUIN.

SERIOUSLY?!
OH GOD...
ITANO DIDN'T YET REALIZE IT, BUT THIS WOULD PROVE AN OPPORTUNITY.

A CHANCE TO FIND THE NEW FORM OF EXPRESSION HE'D BEEN SEARCHING FOR.

RMMMMBLL

EPISODE 20

KRASH
ザラ
KRASH
ザラ

タタタ…
DASHH
THERE YOU ARE!
WHAT ARE YOU DOING OUT HERE, ITANO?!
THE STUDIO'S IN A TIZZY AFTER YASUHIKO'S COLLAPSE!
コーン
KLANG
コーン
KLANG

I'M HERE FOR THE SMOKE.
SKRCH
SKRCH
EPISODE 20

ER, COME AGAIN?
CRRK
I'VE GOTTA WATCH IT UP CLOSE.
CRRAK
OOPSIE-DAISY...
FRSSSHHH
BSSSHOOM
!!!
KRRK
KRRRK

FWSSHOOOM

YOU GOT A DEATH WISH, DUMBASS?!

ITANO...
ゲホ、ゲホ
KOFF KOFF
RGH!

RRMMMMBBL

AH, LOOK AT THAT MOVEMENT.
RMMMBL
GIVES ME CHILLS.
HE ALMOST KILLED HIMSELF JUST TO SEE HOW SMOKE MOVES?
RRMMBL
H-HE'S CRAZY!
OKAY, LEMME SEE THOSE IN-BETWEENS!
NIPPON SUNRISE
HURRY! WE'RE OUTTA TIME!
WHAT ABOUT THE ANIMATION DIRECTOR'S CHECKS?
FORGET THAT! HAND 'EM OVER!
FLPP
JESUS, YASUHIKO GOES DOWN, AND WE MIGHT AS WELL HAVE GONE WITH HIM.
HM?

THE HELL'S THE DEAL, ITANO?
HUH?
THIS MOVEMENT ...

THE MOVEMENT ON THE ELMETH'S BIT IS ALL OUTTA WACK!
IT'S TOO FAST! YOU WON'T BE ABLE TO TRACK IT!

I BEG TO DIFFER.

HUH?

WE'VE GOT PRE-LIMINARY MOVEMENT HERE.

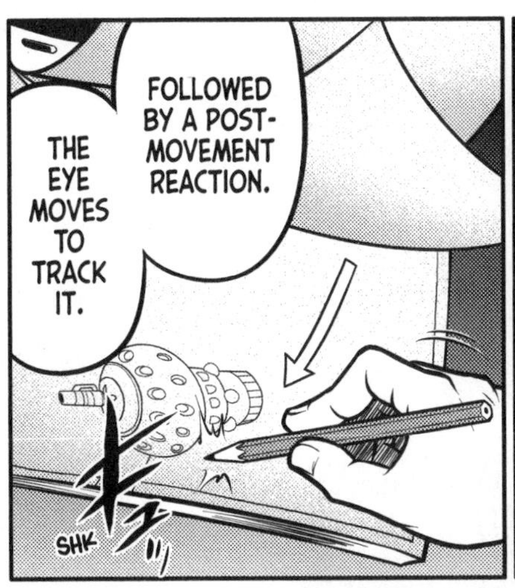
THE EYE MOVES TO TRACK IT.
FOLLOWED BY A POST-MOVEMENT REACTION.
SHK

I TOOK THE RISK NOT TO SPLIT THE MOVEMENT EVENLY.
THE END RESULT GIVES A STUNNING SENSATION OF SPEED.

SKRCH
SKRCH
QUIT SHOOTING FROM THE HIP! I'VE NEVER SEEN ANIMATION LIKE THIS BEFORE!
LET'S JUST TWEAK A FRAME OR THREE HERE, AND...
DUNN
AAH!
OKAY, DONE! LET'S HIT THE BARS!

HOOT
HOOT
NIPPON SUNRISE

KRREAK

SHF

QUIT SHOOTING FROM THE HIP! I'VE NEVER SEEN ANIMATION LIKE THIS BEFORE!
Timing Sheet

IN THAT CASE...

KRRP

I'LL JUST HAVE TO SHOW YOU MYSELF.

CHIRP
CHIRP
OKAY, RUSH TEST SCREENING TIME!
SHFFF
SHUT THE CURTAINS!

HOW'S YASUHIKO'S CONDITION?
HE'S RECUPERATING. STILL NOT READY TO RETURN, THOUGH.
KA-KLAK

I WAS EXPECTING A BAD DRAWING OR TWO, BUT YEESH.
SIGH. NOT FOR LACK OF TRYING, UNFORTUNATELY.

カラカラ...
KA-KLAK

HM?
AH!

カラカラ
KA-KLAK

STOP!
GRRRR
カラカラ
KA-KLAK
I NEVER INSTRUCTED HIM TO—
WAIT. HE WOULDN'T!

WHO DID THE KEY ANIMATION ON THIS?
RMMMBL
KRRK
I DID.

I REWROTE THE TIMING SHEET WHILE THE EPISODE DIRECTOR WAS OUT DRINKING.

HE'S ALWAYS REWORKED MY TIMINGS BEFORE.

ITANO, YOU LITTLE TWERP!

RTTL

SHFF

RRMMMBL

TIME TO LOOK FOR A JOB IN MOTOR-CYCLES...

NICE MOVES, KID.

HUH?

ざわ
MRRMR

WHY THE HELL DIDN'T YOU LET HIM WORK HIS MAGIC?
B-BUT SIR, THE WAY HE DOES THINGS, THEY'VE NEVER BEEN DONE BEFORE!

OPEN UP YOUR EYES, PRICK. *GUNDAM* IS ALL ABOUT DESTROYING THE CONVENTIONS OF TV ANIME.
シュボ
SHFF
SO QUIT DOING SHIT THE WAY IT'S ALWAYS BEEN DONE.
ギロ
GRRR
S-SIR!

GRRT

RAAR

RAAR

RAAR

YOSHIKAZU YASUHIKO'S WITHDRAWAL FROM THE FRONT LINES LED TO LOWER QUALITY ANIMATION, YES.

THEIR WORK HAD A CERTAIN UNREFINED CHARM TO IT.

BUT IT ALSO GAVE YOUNG ANIMATORS A CHANCE TO SPREAD THEIR WINGS.

SKRCH
NO ONE'LL NOTICE...

AT TIMES, HOWEVER, THE RECKLESSNESS OF YOUTH ALSO MADE ITSELF KNOWN.

INCLUDING A PARTICULAR SCENE FROM "ESCAPE," THE FINAL EPISODE.

SQULLLCH

OOOGH...

LADY KYCILIA'S HEAD CAME CLEAN OFF!

*DUE TO ITS SHOCKING NATURE, THIS FOOTAGE HAS BEEN CENSORED.

SHF

WHO DID THIS?

ME.

I MADE SURE TO CAPTURE
THE VISCERA DISCHARGE AS HER BODY GETS TORN APART. ALL IN THE PURSUIT OF REALISM.

YOU OVERDID IT, DUMBASS!

OOF...

THE SCENE WAS ULTIMATELY DEEMED TOO GRISLY AND WAS CLEANED UP PRIOR TO AIRING.

ITANO WOULD AGAIN HANDLE KEY ANIMATION ON THE TOMINO-DIRECTED *IDEON*.

THERE, HE WOULD ANIMATE THE LEGENDARY ADIGO MECHA BATTLE IN EPISODE 29.

AND ON *MACROSS*, HIS TALENTS EXPLODED INTO THE VIOLENT GLORY OF THE "ITANO CIRCUS."

MECHA ACTION WOULD NEVER BE THE SAME AGAIN.

BUT THAT'S A STORY FOR ANOTHER TIME.

THE MEN WHO CREATED
GUNDAM

Itano: Episode 28, "Across the Atlantic Ocean," really left an impression. Tomino brought the finished storyboard over to Yoshikazu's desk, and when they finished reading through it they were both in tears. They were blubbering like babies, saying "This is such a good episode," and "Let's knock it out of the park!" Meanwhile, I was over here wondering what was wrong with these two men.

Once they left, I snuck a peek at the storyboard, and sure enough... I bawled like a baby. *(laughs)* They were truly invested in the show and were trying to create something new. This wasn't a story for kids. They were trying to tell a tale of powerless people caught in the crossfire of war.

Yasuhiko: I wasn't in charge of the episode with Miharu, or the scenes where Amuro's dad shows up, or where Amuro encounters Lalah. If I read the storyboard for an important scene and fell in love with a particular moment, I'd ask to work on it, even if I hadn't been assigned. One of the perks of being animation director. So, I read the storyboard for that one and couldn't help myself. Just a great story.

Even I've got my limits, though, so I couldn't work on everything.

Yasuhiko isn't credited as key animation director for episode 28, but instead oversaw the entire series, similar to a chief animation director in modern parlance.

Itano lamented his ability to animate people, but as you saw earlier in the story, his grasp of timing and movement in scenes like the ones involving the Elmeth's bits was impeccable, earning him eventual renown as a master of mecha animation. He also handled the flamingo scene in the second movie, *Soldiers of Sorrow*.

Yasuhiko: It was a 240-frame animation sheet, which, back then, those were the largest. 100s were standard size. But Itano just slaved away drawing those flamingos. Eventually I started to feel bad for him... *(laughs)* I asked him if he was getting paid extra for it, and he told me, "Nah, same amount." *(laughs)*

Itano: I was still working my way up from the bottom rung. I like to think of it as a learning experience. *(laughs)*

The skills that allowed Itano to draw all those flamingos would pay dividends once it came time for him to work on the action scenes in *Space Runaway Ideon* and *Macross*. He would eventually go on to work as both director and animation director on countless shows. In recent years, he's been hard at work mentoring the next generation of animators. ◆

Ichiro Itano handled the scene in which a flock of flamingos flies by the White Base.

Ichiro Itano

Gundam Front Tokyo Special Night #2 - The Birth of *Mobile Suit Gundam* + Animator Yoshikazu Yasuhiko Exhibit - Talk Show w/ Yoshikazu Yasuhiko, Ichiro Itano & Ryosuke Hikawa

▲ Yoshikazu Yasuhiko (L) and Ichiro Itano (R). They described the studio at the time as having the feel of a family-run backstreet workshop.

Ichiro Itano, who appears in the back half of this story, is based on the real animator of the same name. Renowned for the "Itano Circus," a thrillingly virtuosic showcase of mecha action made famous in *Super Dimensional Fortress Macross*, Itano's work has had a major influence on robot anime. The real Itano, like the fictional one, worked on *Mobile Suit Gundam*, with Yoshikazu Yasuhiko serving as something of a mentor figure.

On Friday, July 12, 2013, a talk show event with Yasuhiko and Itano was held at Gundam Front Tokyo. The two animators waxed nostalgic about their past work, told firsthand stories of shared struggle in the animators' bullpen, and touched on the episode with Miharu that comes up in the manga.

THE MEN WHO CREATED
GUNDAM

EPISODE 21

1981 AND SPRING HAS SPRUNG.

AND *GUNDAM* WAS SCREENED FOR THE MOVIE EXECS.

KA-KLAK カラ

KA-KLAK カラ

THE PRESIDENT OF SHOCHIKU IS SAID TO HAVE UTTERED THE FOLLOWING WORDS…

KA-KLAK カラ

KA-KLAK カラ

WELL, I'LL BE DAMNED.
HRM?

I COULD TELL THE MINUTE THE PROJECTOR STARTED ROLLING.
GUNDAM'S NO ORDINARY ANIME.

EPISODE
21

機動戦士
ガンダム

青春の熱い魂に出逢える——この瞬間に未来は、はじまった。
いま、宇宙世紀の一大叙事詩として映画化！

OH, WOW!

THOSE ARE THE POSTERS? THEY LOOK INCREDIBLE!

YEP. HIS ARTISTRY NEVER FAILS TO IMPRESS.

IS THIS WHERE TEAM *GUNDAM'S* STATIONED?
ER...
HM? SHOCHIKU'S PRESIDENT DIDN'T CONTACT YOU?
FLP
LET'S SEE... OH!
THERE IT IS. TADAHIKO NOBE. SAYS YOU'LL BE WORKING WITH US, STARTING TODAY.
GLAD TO BE HERE!
SO? WHERE SHOULD OL' UNCLE NOBE PUT HIS BAGS?
NYA

WHAT'S HIS STORY?
IT SAYS HE'S AN ADVERTISING PRODUCER.
SEEMS LIKE HE'S FROM THE MOVIE STUDIO.
HMM. GOT THE AIR OF A BIG SHOT ABOUT HIM.

NOBE, WAS IT?
WHAT DID YOU WORK ON PREVIOUSLY?
HM? OH, YOU KNOW. *YAMATO.*
NO KIDDING, *YAMA*—

WAIT, *YAMATO* ?!
THAT *YAMATO* ?!
GONG
WHAT, YOU THINK I WAS STATIONED ON THE COMBINED FLEET?
I'M TALKING ABOUT THE SPACE BATTLESHIP, MY FRIEND!

GOOD LORD...
MRRMR
I GUESS WE'RE IN THE MOVIE BUSINESS.

AT THE TIME, NIPPON SUNRISE WAS JUST ANOTHER FLEDGLING STUDIO. THEY SIMPLY DIDN'T HAVE THE KNOWHOW TO RELEASE A FEATURE FILM.

BUT SHOCHIKU WAS IN THE SAME BOAT. THEY DIDN'T KNOW THE FIRST THING ABOUT MAKING ANIME.
NOBE, WITH ANIME AND FILM EXPERIENCE ALIKE, WAS A NATURAL CHOICE.
...
NOW I GET IT.
THAT SLY FOX OF A PRESIDENT'S GOT ONE HELL OF A HEAD ON HIS SHOULDERS.

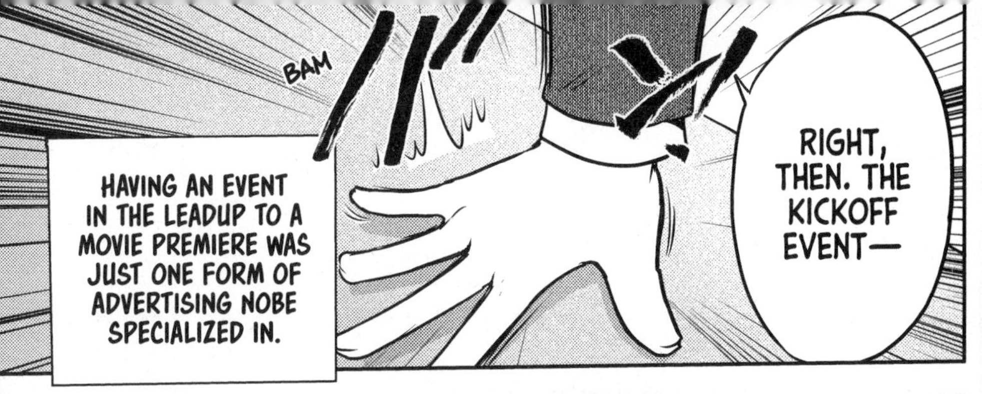

BAM
RIGHT, THEN. THE KICKOFF EVENT—
HAVING AN EVENT IN THE LEADUP TO A MOVIE PREMIERE WAS JUST ONE FORM OF ADVERTISING NOBE SPECIALIZED IN.

LET'S START THINGS OFF WITH A BANG, SHALL WE?
HA HA!
I'M ALL ABOUT STARTING THINGS OFF WITH BANGS.
MAKE IT A BIG ONE.
YOU'VE GOT IT!
HA HA HA!
...

VRRROOM

UM, MR. NOBE?

WORRIED ABOUT OUR LACK OF BUDGET, RIGHT?

A MOVIE IS NOTHING WITHOUT THE WORK ITSELF, CERTAINLY.

BUT IT'S ALSO AN EVENT. A FESTIVAL.

A FESTIVAL?

THAT'S RIGHT. THE HOTTER A FESTIVAL'S FLAMES OF PASSION BURN, THE MORE PEOPLE FIND THEMSELVES IRRESISTIBLY DRAWN TO IT.

AND WHEN THEY ARRIVE, THEY'LL HAPPILY FORK OVER THE TICKET FEE.

FWOOOSH

OHH...

HAHAHA! NO NEED TO WORRY. STARTING A FIRE WITHOUT KINDLING IS A CHALLENGE,

BUT WE'RE POURING OIL ON A RAGING BLAZE.

AND I'VE BEEN WATCHING IT BURN THIS WHOLE TIME.

HONK
HONK
HUH? THE EDITOR-IN-CHIEF?
Animec
EDITORIAL

HE'S OUT OF COMMISSION AT THE MOMENT.
FULL-ON *GUNDAM* BRAIN. NOT GOOD FOR MUCH ELSE.
WE'RE HERE ON *GUNDAM* BUSINESS, ACTUALLY.
ARE YOU? HEAD ON UPSTAIRS, THEN.
KREAK
KRRRK
SHIING
BOOOM

ROOOAR

RMMMBBL

JUST AS I THOUGHT. THERE'S FIRE HERE.

GUNDAM FANS WERE FREQUENT VISITORS TO *ANIMEC* EDITORIAL.

IT WAS THE HEART OF THE *GUNDAM* MOVEMENT, FOR ALL INTENTS AND PURPOSES.

...WITH THAT IN MIND, WE'D LIKE TO THROW A PROMO EVENT.

JUST ONE PROBLEM. WE DON'T HAVE ANY CASH.

MRRMR

!!!

NOBE SPOKE OPENLY ABOUT THE BUDGET ISSUE.

AND IT WORKED.

SHOOOM

WHICH BRINGS US TO WHY WE'RE HERE.

WE NEED HELP.

YOU THERE. DON'T YOU WANT TO SEE NEW CUTS BY YOSHIKAZU YASUHIKO HIMSELF?
HUH ?!

RRMMMBBLL
I... I...
GOSH GOLLY DO I EVER, SIR!
GWAR

RIGHT?
UNFORTUNATELY, THIS IS NO SURE THING.
Animec

IF *PART I* DOES POORLY, OUR HARD-FOUGHT *PART II* COULD END UP ON THE CHOPPING BLOCK.

BAMM

S-SAY IT AIN'T SO!

HUSSHHH

BUT IF OUR KICKOFF EVENT GOES WELL, THE MEDIA WILL EAT IT UP.

AND MORE EXPOSURE MEANS BIGGER BOX OFFICE.

WE HAVE TO MAKE THIS A SUCCESS. PERIOD.

RRMMMBLL

HMM.

WE WANT TO KNOW WHAT YOU'RE THINKING FROM A FAN PERSPECTIVE. IF YOU HAVE ANY IDEAS, PLEASE, SHARE THEM.

MRRMR

KLAK

EXCUSE ME!

I BELIEVE *GUNDAM* FAILED ON TV BECAUSE IT STRUGGLED TO WIN OVER CHILDREN.

AS SUCH, WE SHOULD GO BACK TO BASICS,

AND TRY TO APPEAL MORE TO KIDS!

GREAT IDEA!

WHAT SHOULD WE DO?

SNAPP

HOW ABOUT... A *GUNDAM* DRAWING SONG?

SKRCH
THEN YOU HAVE A HARO.
DUNN
AW, I'M ALREADY DONE!
I LOVE IT! JUST WONDERFUL!
HA HA HA!
KEEP THE IDEAS COMING, EVERY-ONE!
SUGGEST ANYTHING YOU LIKE.
UNCLE NOBE WILL SHOULDER THE RESPONSI-BILITY.
SOUNDS GOOD!

YEAHHH! WOOOO!
BY THE BY, THERE WAS SOMETHING I WANTED TO DISCUSS.
OH?

IF YOU MOBILIZED THE FANS, LET'S SAY, HOW MANY WOULD SHOW UP?

ANIMEC EDITORIAL KEEPS CLOSE TABS ON FAN GROUPS NATIONWIDE.
FLP
COUNTING FANS WHO'D BE ABLE TO SHOW UP AT A MOMENT'S NOTICE...
CHK
ABOUT A THOUSAND!
A THOUSAND! WONDERFUL! MORE THAN I COULD HAVE ASKED FOR.
HA HA HA!
WHAT DO YOU WANNA CALL THEM IN FOR?

A FESTIVAL.
ONE THAT WILL ANNOUNCE THE START OF *ANIME'S NEW CENTURY*.
SHHHNG
"ANIME'S NEW CENTURY"?
THE LOCATION WILL BE SOMEWHERE WITH CONSIDERABLE FOOT TRAFFIC. FOR EXAMPLE ...
THE LARGEST TRAIN STATION IN JAPAN. NO, THE WORLD.

RRMMMMBL
IN FRONT OF SHINJUKU ALTA.
STUDIO ALTA

WHEN KOMAKI HEARD THESE WORDS
"ANIME'S NEW CENTURY"...
KCHK
HE COULD FEEL AN INDESCRIBABLE FEELING OF ELATION WELLING UP FROM THE VERY CORE OF HIS BEING.
ONLY A FEW COLD WINTER DAYS REMAINED UNTIL FEBRUARY 22, 1981.
RMMMBL

EPISODE
22
チュン CHIRP
チュン CHIRP
NIPPON SUNRISE

FWAA...
WELL, THAT'S ANOTHER ALL-NIGHTER IN THE BOOKS.
BWAAH
MY BODY'S ABOUT TO IMPLODE.
チャッ CHK

にゅ〜〜 GLOOOP

EPISODE 22
...
PEEK
UH. CHIEF?

RRMMMBLL
HEY! ITANO!
THE HELL'S GOIN' ON HERE?!
THE TOOTHPASTE'S ALL STRIPEY!

GRRP
AAGH!
HOLY SHIT! IT'S STRIPIN', END TO END!
MY AQUA-FRESH!
BLOOOP

The New Anime Century Declaration

BAM

機動戦士ガンダム

Poster: 2/22 New Anime Century Declaration Ceremony. 500 Animation Cel Lottery Giveaway.Record advance ticket sales!
In Shochiku theaters nationwide Saturday, March 14!

THE NEW ANIME CENTURY DECLARATION?

THAT'S RIGHT.

IT'S WHAT IT SAYS ON THE TIN.

AN ANNOUNCEMENT OF ANIME'S NEW CENTURY.

THE SQUARE OUTSIDE SHINJUKU STATION'S EAST EXIT? YOU DON'T MEAN...

RIGHT IN FRONT OF ALTA.

I WANTED TO RENT OUT STUDIO ALTA ENTIRELY, AND REALLY BLOW THE DOORS OFF WITH A LIVE BROADCAST.

BUT, YOU KNOW. NO BUDGET.

HM?

WAIT A MINUTE...

BAM

アニメ新世紀宣言大会

2月22日(日)午後1時~3時

IT SAYS ME, TOMINO, AND OKAWARA WILL BE THERE. AND WE'LL BE SIGNING AUTOGRAPHS?!

INDEED. YOU'RE PRACTICALLY IDOLS TO THE FANBASE.

ABSOLUTELY NOT! WE DON'T HAVE TIME IN THE SCHEDULE!

Poster: The New Anime Century Declaration. Feb. 22 (Sun) - 1-3 p.m. Location... 1. Intro with Tomino, Yasuhiko, Okawara, and the voice actors. 3. Gundam Festival Fashion Contest: Best 10 will win signed king size...

LOOK AT THIS! VISITORS GET FREE POSTERS!

WOW, 5,000 FREE–

WAIT, FIVE THOUSAND?!

MRRMR

ざわざわ

THIS IS NUTS.

ALTA WAS KEY.
ROOOOAR
Note: B&B was a manzai comedy duo formed in 1972.
READY, SET!
AT THE TIME, THERE WERE FEW BETTER PLACES TO REACH THE PUBLIC.
B&B
B&B

ROOOOAR
IT'S A LAUGHING MATTER!
AH HA HA HA!
THIS WAS THE FIERY EPICENTER OF AN EXPLOSIVE MANZAI COMEDY BOOM, WITH LIVE TV AS THE MAIN DELIVERY MECHANISM.
RARR
RARR
THE AREA IN FRONT OF ALTA WAS PRACTICALLY A FESTIVAL GROUNDS MOST DAYS OF THE WEEK.
IT WAS A LOCATION THAT DEFINED A GENERATION.
BUT THAT' ALSO WHA MADE IT DANGEROU
SHINJUKU STATION WAS THE WORLD'S LARGEST TRAIN HUB, WITH 700,000 PEOPLE CROWDING ITS HALLS DAILY.
ONE WRONG STEP COULD TRANSFORM THE CROWD INTO AN ANGRY MOB.

Note: *It's a Laughing Matter*, (*Waratteru Baai Desuyo!*) was a variety show that ran from 1980 to 1982 on Fuji TV. It was filmed inside Studio ALTA.

THE CHALLENGE ALTA PRESENTS IS PRECISELY WHAT MAKES THIS WORTHWHILE.
KSHNK
カタッ

HOLDING THE EVENT NEAR THE THEATER WOULD, IN FACT, BE EASIER.
THE MORNING EVENT IS EFFECTIVELY INSURANCE.
BUT IT WON'T BE ENOUGH ON ITS OWN!
FROM ON HIGH, WE'LL DECLARE A SIMPLE, UNDENIABLE FACT TO THE MASSES!
GUNDAM IS THE NEXT GENERATION OF ANIME!

RRMMMBL

WHEN I ENCOUNTER A TRULY REMARKABLE WORK, I CAN'T HELP BUT WANT TO SHOUT IT FROM THE ROOFTOPS.

IT'S PROBABLY WHY I'M WORKING IN THE MOVIES.

REGARDLESS, I'LL BE TAKING FULL RESPONSIBILITY.
SHF

WORST CASE, I'LL SLIT MY BELLY WIDE OPEN.

THAT'S WHY I WAS SENT HERE, AFTER ALL.

BMPF

NO SEPPUKU ...

IF YOU'RE THAT SERIOUS ABOUT THIS WHOLE THING, I'M DEFINITELY NOT GONNA COMPLAIN.
WHAT'S NEXT?

ガタ
KSHF
YASU-HIKO!

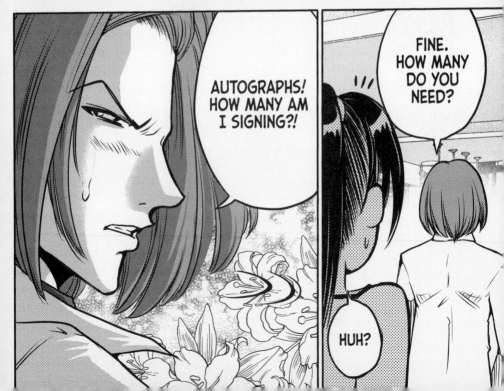

FINE. HOW MANY DO YOU NEED?

HUH?

AUTOGRAPHS! HOW MANY AM I SIGNING?!

HEH. WHAT A BOY SCOUT.

2.22アニメ新世紀宣言大会
THE NEW ANIME CENTURY DECLARATION WAS ADVERTISED IN THE PAGES OF THE *YOMIURI SHIMBUN*. A NEW EXPERIMENT FOR THE ANIME INDUSTRY.
FANS ACROSS THE NATION WOULD BE COMING TO THE EVENT.
WHEN INSIDERS SAW THIS, THEIR BLOOD RAN COLD.
AND THAT SAME DAY...
ドォオオン
BWOOOOM
WAAUGH!

Note: *Yomiuri Shimbun* is one of Tokyo's premier daily newspapers.

THE LONG-AWAITED REBROADCAST BEGAN IN THE KANTO AREA!
RATINGS IMMEDIATELY TRIPLED.

THE ADULTS THOUGHT THEY COULDN'T HANDLE IT. THEY WERE WRONG.
AND KIDS ATE UP THE STORY, IMMERSING THEMSELVES IN THE WORLD OF GUNDAM.

SHNNNG
THE TIME WAS RIPE INDEED.

FEBRUARY 21ST, 1981 SHINJUKU.
KLANG
KLANG
KLANG
SHINJUKU STATION

KLANG
カーン
KLANG
カーン
KLANG
カーン
VRREEEE
キイイイ
VRWWRR
ウイイーン
VRWWRR
ブゥウゥウン
2/22
NEW ANIME CENTU
CLARATION CEREMON
GUNDAM
IN THEATERS
MARCH 14
GRRRR
ガガガガ…

LOOK AT THE SIZE OF IT! DAMN, YOU GUYS OUTDID YOURSELVES!
I WANTED TO PUT UP A LIFE-SIZE VERSION.
THE AUTHORITIES WOULDN'T LET US GO OVER 10 METERS, THOUGH.
AH, IF ONLY!
AN 18-METER GUNDAM... ONE DAY, WE'LL SEE IT RISE IN FRONT OF OUR EYES.
DAMN RIGHT WE WILL.
RUSHH
HANDLE THINGS OVER THERE FOR A BIT!
I'M HEADING BACK TO *ANIMEC* EDITORIAL!
OKAY!

GOOD-NESS! BUSY, BUSY!
NOBE, QUESTION!

IS THE SCRIPT FOR THE DECLAR-ATION READY?
JUST A LITTLE LONGER, NOW!

YOU'RE STILL TWEAKING IT?!
WE NEED TIME TO MAKE COPIES, Y'KNOW!

WELL AWARE. BUT WE HAVE TO GET THIS RIGHT.
JUST A LITTLE MORE, OKAY?

THE SOONER THE BETTER.

HUH?
SOME-THING AMISS?

THERE'S SOMETHING OFF ABOUT THOSE PEOPLE OVER THERE.
THAT CORNER OVER THERE, TOO.

OH MY GOSH. ARE THEY WAITING FOR THE DECLARATION?
HAHA, DON'T BE RIDICULOUS. THE EVENT AT ALTA IS TOMORROW AFTERNOON.

YEAH, YOU'RE RIGHT.
CHOP CHOP ON THE SCRIPT! GOT A LOT TO TAKE CARE OF, Y'KNOW!
IT'S IN GOOD HANDS.

SOON ENOUGH...
BKOOOM
0:00
FEBRUARY 22ND, 1981 WAS AT HAND.

AS THE SUN ROSE ON THIS FATEFUL DAY,

IT BECAME CLEAR TO EVERYONE

THAT THIS WOULD BE NO ORDINARY EVENT.

EPISODE 23
CHIRP
チュン
CHIRP
チュン
HIC! NOTHING LIKE DRINKIN' 'TILL THE SUN COMES UP! WOO!
YOU'VE HAD TOO MUCH, SIR! YOUR WIFE WILL BE FURIOUS!
AW, SHADDUP! I DRINK TO ESCAPE THE FEAR–
HUH?
THD
THD
THD
WHAT THE?
THD

EPISODE
23
THDDD

SHONAN WHITE BASE SURE IS RUNNING LATE.
THE FOLKS FROM CHIBA SIDE 7 SHOULD BE HERE ANY MINUTE.
THD
WHEN DOES THE GUNDAM FASHION SHOW START?
WE STILL HAVE TIME. SEEMS LIKE WE'RE EARLY.
THD
WH- WHAT ARE THEY?!
THE IDEA OF *COSPLAY* HAD YET TO PENETRATE THE PUBLIC CONSCIOUSNESS.
IT WAS SOMETHING PERFORMED OUT OF SIGHT, AT SMALL EVENTS, BY ENTHUSIASTS ONLY.

HUH?

CHIEF, LOOK AT THAT!

GUNDAM WAS THE FIRST TIME IT HAD BEEN BROUGHT OUT INTO THE OPEN.

WHAT ARE ALL THOSE PEOPLE DOING OUT HERE THIS EARLY?

ざわ MRRMR

ざわ MRRMR

WHAT IN GOD'S NAME IS ABOUT TO HAPPEN?! HEY?!

MR. KOMAKIII!
CAN I HELP YOU?
HAAH
HAAH
PEOPLE ARE ALREADY GATHERING OUTSIDE ALTA.

PSHHK
HAH HAH! WELL, THIS IS THE FIRST EVENT LIKE THIS SINCE *YAMATO.* THE FANS ARE RARIN' TO GO.
HOW MANY ARE THERE?
LOOKS TO BE AROUND 2,000 PEOPLE OR SO.
GLG
GLG
NO KIDDING? 2,000 PEOP—

PSHOOO
TWO THOUSAND?!
WAA-AAA-UGH!

R-
REALLY?!
YEAH! AND THEY'RE STILL SHOWING UP!
HOORAY! SOUNDS LIKE THE EVENT'S GONNA BE A BIG SUCCESS!
WOOOOO
HELL YEAH!

WHAT GREAT NEWS! WE CAN REST EASY NOW AND–
WOO YEAAH
RMMMMBLLL

IS SOMETHING WRONG, NOBE?

AM I THE ONLY ONE WITH A SENSE OF FOREBODING ABOUT THIS?

ゴゴゴゴ

RMMMMBLLL

THE DAY'S BARELY STARTED, AND 2,000 PEOPLE ARE ALREADY LINED UP.

HOW BIG WILL THAT NUMBER BE ONCE IT'S ACTUALLY TIME?

WE HAVE TO DO SOME-THING!
WHAT ABOUT THE FANZINE KIDS?
THEY'VE BEEN MOBILIZED, SO I THINK WE CAN EXPECT QUITE A FEW OF THEM!
LET'S HEAD OUT THERE AND MANAGE THE CROWD! DON'T FORGET THE ROPE!
SHOOM
R-RIGHT!
IF YOU'RE NOT BUSY, I WANT YOU AT THE EVENT SITE!
KLAP
KLAP
CHOP CHOP!
ZOOOM
TH-THIS IS CRAZY!
I ONLY PRAY YOU MAKE IT IN TIME.

新宿松竹会館

AN EVENT WAS HELD AT SHOCHIKU'S SHINJUKU THEATER IN THE MORNING.

SEATING WAS LIMITED TO A LOTTERY, SO IT WENT OFF WITHOUT A HITCH.

RAAR

RAAR

-RUSHH

IN PREPARATION FOR THE EVENT, A SECURITY DETAIL WAS DEPLOYED IN FRONT OF ALTA.

AN ULTIMATELY FUTILE GESTURE.

XII

KLIK

SEIKO

WHY, YOU ASK? BECAUSE THE NUMBER OF FANS THAT ARRIVED...

BWOOOON

SEIKO

STUDIO ALTA

BWOOOON

BWOOON
BWOOON
EXCEEDED ESTIMATES BY 1,000%.
SHHF
THAT'S RIGHT.
BWOOOON
BWOOOON

THE CROWD HAD BALLOONED TO OVER 20,000 PEOPLE.

ドォォォ
BOOOOOOOM

RAAR
GAH, WHERE'S THE BATHROOM?!
HEY! STAY OFF THE EMBANKMENT!
RAAR
WE ARE OUT OF POSTERS. I REPEAT...
SIEG ZEON!
SIEG!
RAAR
THEY STILL HAVEN'T STARTED?!
PLEASE REFRAIN FROM PUSHING.
OW!
RAAR

BWSHAAAH
MY WORD ...
WHAT INCREDIBLE PRESSURE!
THIS MAY BE A NIGHTMARE IN THE MAKING WE'RE WALKING INTO.
NYA. HA.

*Note: Piss Alley was a collection of bars by Shinjuku Station's west exit.

FWOOOOSH
THIS WAS TRULY AN HISTORIC DAY.
SHINJUKU HAD BEEN COMPLETELY TAKEN OVER BY GUNDAM FANS!
HEY, YASUHIKO! DRAW SAYLA FOR ME!
RAAAH
RAAAH
COOL! ALL THE V.A. REGULARS ARE HERE!
RAAAH
RAAAH
OH MY GOD! IT'S FURUYA!
RAAAH
HEY, THIS IS KINDA... NUTS, ISN'T IT?
RAAAH
YEAH...
RAAAH
RAAAH

HEY! PLEASE, NO PUSHING!
RAAAAH
RAAAAH
RAAAAH
GRRK
ROOOOOAR
HUFF
HUFF
DON'T— OOH, ACTUALLY...
BWOOOING

BEEP
BEEP
BEEP
BSHAAAAA
HEY!
YA TRYIN' TO GET RUN OVER?!
BAAM
STAY OFF THE ROAD!
RARR
RARR
I REPEAT, STAY OFF THE ROAD!
BEEP
BWAAH
THIS ISN'T GOOD.
WHAT I FEARED IS COMING TO PASS.
RAAR
RAAR
RAAR
RAAR

YASU-HIKO!
DIRECTOR TOMINO!
RAAR
DAMMIT, OUT OF THE WAY!
RAAR
IS THE ORGANIZER PRESENT?
ER, YES!
ARGH, I CAN'T HOLD 'EM BACK!
IT'S ALL OVER!
GRRRRK
GRK

THIS EVENT IS CANCELLED! DISPERSE IMMEDIATELY!
RRMMMBBL
AT THIS RATE, WE'RE GONNA HAVE AN INCIDENT ON OUR HANDS.
CALL OFF THE EVENT IMMEDIATELY!

TRMBL
OH NO...
TRMBL
NO! IT CAN'T END LIKE THIS!
RAAR
ROOOOOOOAR
PLP
PLP
ANIME'S NEW CENTURY IS GONNA END BEFORE IT EVEN BEGINS!
S- SOMEBODY...
ANYBODY!

FINAL EPISODE
ROOOOAR
W-WE'RE DOOMED! SOMEBODY, SAVE US!
RAHH
RAHH
ANY-BODY!

DON'T MOVE!!

しーん…
HUSSSSHHH
AT THAT INSTANT …
FOR THE FIRST TIME SINCE ALTA WAS BUILT
IT WAS QUIET ENOUGH TO HEAR A PIN DROP.
XII
SEIKO
K CHK
STUDIO ALTA
THE CROWD'S ATTENTION WAS FIXATED ON THE STAGE.
OR RATHER …
THE MAN STANDING UPON IT.
ゴゴゴ
RRMMMMBBBLL

BWOOOSSSH

ザ

DI...
RECTOR...
RRMMBL

T-
TOMINO?

STAY RIGHT WHERE YOU ARE!

I SEE YOU TAKE SO MUCH AS ONE STEP, AND YOU'RE DEAD!

MRRMR

IS THIS A GATHERING OF BRAINDEAD IDIOTS?! WHAT IF SOMEBODY GETS HURT?!

SOCIETY'S GONNA LOOK AT THIS AND SAY, "SEE? GET A BUNCH OF ANIME FREAKS IN ONE PLACE, AND ALL HELL BREAKS LOOSE!"

WE HAVE TO MAKE THIS FESTIVAL A SUCCESS!

FAIL, AND *GUNDAM* ENDS RIGHT HERE, RIGHT NOW!

ざわ MRRMR

GUNDAM'S GONNA... END?!

HAHH

HAHH

SHP

TAKE A GOOD LOOK AROUND YOU.

THE PEOPLE IN YOUR MIDST DON'T HATE *GUNDAM*.

THEY SURE AS HELL AIN'T YOUR ENEMY!

YOU'RE ALLIES! EVERY GODDAMN ONE OF YOU!

ざわ…
MRRMR
ピキイイン
ZIIIING
BAAAAM
YOU LIKE GUNDAM TOO?
にっ
NYA
YUP!

SHFF
THE PRESSURE FROM THE MOB! IT'S RELENTING!
SHFF
TH—
THEIR AWARENESS, IT'S—
FWMP

ZIING
THEY'RE ALLIES... RIGHT.
THAT'S RIGHT!
THEIR AWARENESS...
IT'S EXPANDING!
OF COURSE.
FWAAAAAH
EVERYONE FEELS THE SAME WAY!

HEY, KOMAKI.
THE ROPE...
WE NO LONGER REQUIRE SUCH THINGS.

ALERT!! 2/22 NEW ANIME CENTURY DECLARATION CEREMONY
MOBILE SUIT GUNDAM
IN THEATERS MARCH 14
WE, FOR THE FIRST TIME, HAVE AN ANIME TO CALL OUR OWN.
MOBILE SUIT GUNDAM
IS A NEWTYPE ANIME THAT BLURS THE LINE BETWEEN CREATOR AND AUDIENCE.
THIS IS A WORK
DEPICTING A PALPABLY REAL FUTURE OF MAN INTERMINGLED WITH MACHINE.
I TOLD YOU TO MAKE A SHOW TO SELL TOYS TO CHILDREN!

THE CHARACTERS SUFFER.
THEY STRUGGLE ALONG IN THE DARK ABSURDITY OF WAR, EVERY BREATH A MIRACLE.
THERE, LOVE AND TRUTH ARE TOO DISTANT TO BE SEEN.
YET IN TIME, THEY ARRIVE AT THE FAINTEST GLIMMER OF HOPE— A NEWTYPE AWAKENING.
SOMETHING THAT SEEMS ALL BUT IMPOSSIBLE TO US IN THE REAL WORLD.
WHY?
BECAUSE AMURO'S AWAKENING BELONGS TO HIM AND HIM ALONE.
You hit me again?! Even my father never hit me!

THIS IS A DRAMA THAT QUESTIONS THE MEANING OF LIFE ITSELF.
IF WE ARE TO ACCEPT THIS QUESTION, WE MUST DO SO WITH PROFOUND EXPECTATION AND RESOLVE.
LET ME AUDITION FOR THIS CHAR GUY.
WE MUST SEEK A NEWTYPE AWAKENING OF OUR OWN.
TO USHER IN THE DAWN OF OUR ERA, WITH ANIME ITS GUIDING LIGHT. A NEW ANIME CENTURY!
WE HEREBY DECLARE!

TODAY IS FEBRUARY 22, 0001
OF THE NEW ANIME CENTURY!

ROOOAR

WE'RE GONNA BE BUSY.
RAHH
RAHH

THEY'RE EXPECTING BIG THINGS.
AND WE'VE GOTTA DELIVER.

INDEED WE DO.
THE FESTIVAL WAS OVER.
SOON, THE *GUNDAM* MOVIE WAS RELEASED IN THEATERS.
IT SHATTERED RECORDS AT THE BOX OFFICE.

MOBILE SUIT GUNDAM
BADGES DISTRIBUTED BY SHOCHIKU TO PRODUCTION MEMBERS.
ITS SEQUELS, *SOLDIERS OF SORROW* AND *ENCOUNTERS IN SPACE*, WERE SUCCESSES AS WELL.
RAHH
RAHH

THE *GUNDAM* TRILOGY BECAME AN EPOCHAL MEGA HIT.

SHRRREEE

BUT YOU ALREADY FIGURED THAT OUT, DIDN'T YOU?

EFSF
WB
IT'S HUGE!
YOU BUILT IT, RIGHT, MOM?
OF COURSE NOT, SILLY.
IT'S BEEN 30 YEARS.
I WONDER WHAT TOMINO WOULD SAY IF HE WAS HERE.

IF YOU PIPED UP, IT'D PROBABLY THROW A REAL MONKEY WRENCH IN THE GEARS.

FWWSH

HEH. GOT THAT RIGHT.

OH, HEY!

HARD TO BELIEVE THEY REALLY BUILT A LIFE-SIZE GUNDAM.

HELL OF A FEAT.

NOT QUITE.

IT CAN'T MOVE, LET ALONE FIGHT! DOESN'T EVEN HAVE A CORE FIGHTER!
IT'S JUST A BIG, GUNDAM-SIZED PAPER-WEIGHT!
TALK ABOUT MISPLACED EXPECTATIONS.

IT'LL MOVE. EVENTUALLY.
WHEN?
DECADES... MAYBE A CENTURY FROM NOW.
WB
AIN'T THAT RIGHT?
THEN
NYA
FROM THAT MOMENT FORWARD...

WB
EFSF
GUNDAM BECAME LEGEND.

THE MEN WHO CREATED GUNDAM

FIN

(From top) Yoshiyuki Tomino, Yoshikazu Yasuhiko, and Kunio Okawara greet the fans.

by in front of Shinjuku ALTA, and their numbers only continued to grow. The press could only get an accurate count up to 8,000 people, but those who were there at the time suggest there were anywhere from 10,000 to 15,000 fans present. It was truly unprecedented.

Flanked by the giant Gundam standee on stage, voice actors and staff members held talk shows, raffled off animation cells and posters, and oversaw cosplay and skit competitions. Ultimately, the New Anime Century Declaration was a rousing success, raising awareness of anime's growing cultural cachet, and making the *Gundam* films an even bigger hit.

Like other TV anime series before it, the story of *Gundam* had reached its climax with a film adaptation. Celebrating it in a fashion this festive and exciting put the final, finishing touches on a legend to be remembered for generations to come. ◆

(A side few of the stage, with fans gathered.)

A massive Gundam standee flanked the stage, striking a pose not unlike its life-size successor.

The New Anime Century Declaration

Yomiuri Shimbun, February 6, 1981, evening edition

In February 1981, the New Anime Century Declaration Ceremony was held in the square near Shinjuku Station's east exit, in front of the ALTA Building. This would prove to be a major turning point for *Mobile Suit Gundam*, whose creators wished to see animation promoted and recognized as a cultural work. The declaration ceremony was a place where such ideals, shared by both creators and fans alike, took shape.

On February 6th, the evening edition of the *Yomiuri Shimbun* featured a half-page ad toward the bottom of the television listings. It passionately declared, "We wish to proclaim a New Anime Century with all of you, whose dawning will be ushered in courtesy of the Newtype anime we have created."

Though slightly opaque, the intent behind the ad was to create a sense of unity between creator and viewer, and to spread awareness of animation as culturally valuable work. Of course, the ad also mentions the explosive advance ticket sales for the film. This large-scale marketing push made the event a success, and paved the way for the sequels.

What actually occurred on the ground was far more chaotic, and it was this tumult that ended up in the pages of the *Yomiuri Shimbun* on February 23rd, the day after the event. The Gundam Festival, held in the morning, had limited attendance, and went off without a hitch, just as Tadahiko Nobe promised. However, the fans who had camped out overnight were still standing

Courtesy of: The Yomiuri Shimbun, Shochiku Co., Ltd., Masanobu Komaki

Gundam Parody/Fashion Show

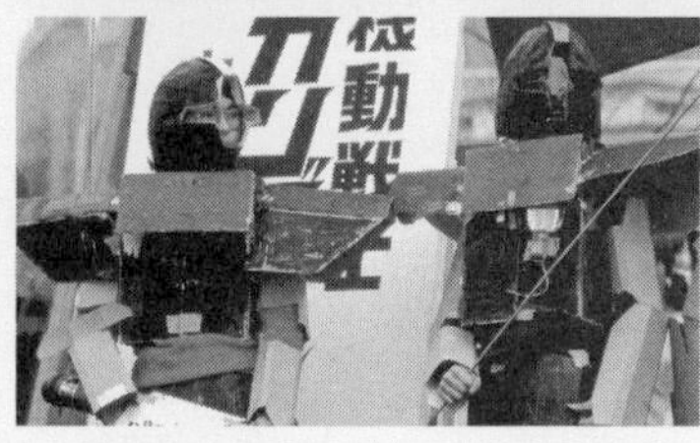

▲ Cosplayers performed short skits and put on a fashion show, with an awards ceremony for best costume.

新宿駅東口広場を埋め尽くしたチビッ子たち ▼

"過熱"に主催者もビックリ

アニメ宣伝に一万人！

少年ら徹夜三百人も

二十二日、新宿駅東口広場は、アニメ・ファンの子供たち約一万人で埋まり、歩行者天国を楽しみにやって来た家族連れたちをびっくりさせた。

子供たちのお目当ては、テレビ放映で人気のアニメ映画「機動戦士ガンダム」の劇場映画化を記念して、映画会社が東口ステーション・スクエアで開いた「2・22アニメ新世紀宣言大会」。仮装ファッションショー、主題歌発表、セル原画五百枚抽選プレゼントなど盛りだくさんの企画に誘われて、さる二十日夕、埼玉県から中学生二人が早々と到着、行列のトップに並んだ。いくらなんでも二日間は、と映画会社側が説得したが、効果なし。翌二十一日になると、行列はふえる一方で、同夜から二十二日朝まで三百五十人が毛布やカイロで暖をとりながら徹夜した。

二十二日になると、小中学生が早朝から続々と大集合、午前七時に二千人に達した。係員はポスターを渡してその数を数えたが、開始時刻の午後一時に八千人まで数えたところで、カウント中止。ふくれ上がる子供たちの整理に全員が追われて数え切れず、最終的な人数は約一万人にのぼったのは確実と見ている。

主人公のアムロ・レイや、アズナブル少佐などにふんした、仮装ファッション参加者たち八十人がステージに現れると、ワーワーと大変な騒ぎ。超過密状態の広場はパンク寸前。危険な事態も考えられるふん囲気となったため、主催者は早めに行事を切り上げ、午後二時すぎ散会した。

この日は日曜日で歩行者天国。新宿署は署員十人を派遣、現場警備に当たったが、地下道から東口に出る人たちは、いきなりこの光景にぶつかって目をパチクリ。警察側がやっと作った通路を身を細めて歩きながら「いったい何の騒ぎ？」と、子供たちの背後で首をひねっていた。

Yomiuri Shimbun, February 23, 1981, noting 10,000 people at the event.

◀ Tomino at the Gundam Festival. That morning, Tomino signed autographs at the Gundam Festival held at Shinjuku Shochiku.

Movie Flyers

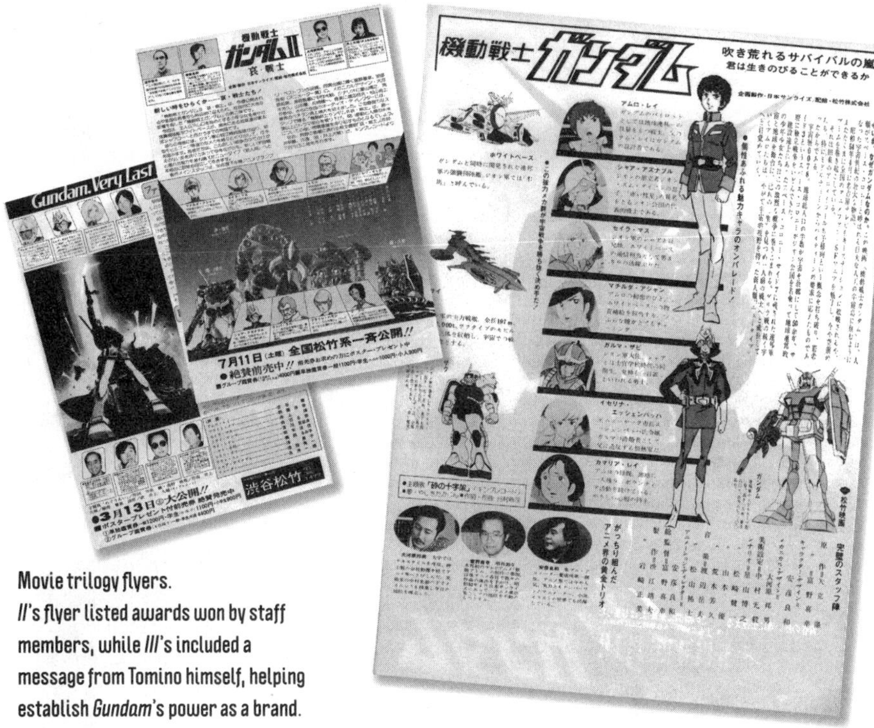

Movie trilogy flyers.
II's flyer listed awards won by staff members, while *III*'s included a message from Tomino himself, helping establish *Gundam*'s power as a brand.

EARLIER IN THE story, we witnessed with amazement as the *Gundam* film sold 10,000 advance tickets, stunning the movie execs, and earning Yoshiyuki Tomino the chance to make his movie trilogy. But one look at the flyers for the film reveals just how precarious the situation was for Tomino and the team.

It all starts with the name of the film: *Mobile Suit Gundam*. No mention of potential sequels is made, and the roman numeral I is nowhere to be found. The sequels hadn't been greenlit yet, which meant the production staff were walking a tightrope where every step could mark the end of *Gundam*'s silver screen ambitions. It was only after fans started lining up for advance tickets that the team found their safety net.

As stated in the monologue at the end of this fictionalized retelling of events, the *Gundam* movies were smash hits, with the flyer for the third film, *Encounters in Space*, serving as a thank-you from Tomino to all the fans who made the trilogy possible. ◆

The Life-Size Gundam

The life-size Gundam on display at Odaiba.

▲▶ The body's fiber-reinforced plastic parts were transported individually and assembled on-site. Once assembled, a steady stream of events kept visitors coming.

The date is July 11, 2009. Here in Odaiba's Shiokaze Park, 30 years after 1979, a new landmark is nearing completion. There can be no mistake...it's a Gundam.

In the story, Tadahiko Nobe speaks of a dream to one day build a life-size Gundam, and this year, in this location, that dream has become a reality. The life-size statue was constructed to celebrate the 30th anniversary of *Mobile Suit Gundam*'s original TV broadcast and was also part of an effort to earn Tokyo the right to host the Olympics (still undecided as of 2009). It was only on display until August 31, 2009, but it still managed to attract a whopping 4.15 million visitors during that brief timeframe.

Afterwards, it was dismantled and reassembled at various events before ending up in front of Higashi-Shizuoka Station, where it stood from July 2010 to January 2011. It moved to Odaiba's Diver City Plaza, where it overlooked Tokyo Bay since the plaza's opening, from April 2012 through August 2017.

At the end of this manga, Yoshiyuki Tomino makes a sarcastic jab at the statue's lack of movement, but there's no denying its awe-inspiring sense of scale. If you ever have the opportunity, you owe it to yourself to visit this 59-foot legend in person. [Editor's note: It's since been replaced by a life-size version of the Unicorn Gundam, while Gundam Factory Yokohama now has a life-size RX-78 that moves.] ◆

GUNDAM GENESIS
THE UNTOLD STORY
PART 1

THE END OF A YEAR, SOMEWHERE, SOMETIME. IT ALL WENT DOWN AT KADOKAWA SHOTEN'S NEW YEAR PARTY...

NEW YEAR'S PARTY

YEAHHH

WHOO

HOW'S IT HANGIN', MR. E-I-C?
YEAH?
MANGA ARTIST HIDEKI
EDITOR-IN-CHIEF MR. I

I WAS WONDERING ABOUT THAT PROJECT, ACTUALLY.

...THAT PROJECT?
YOU MEAN THE MANGA WITH TOMINO AS THE MAIN CHARACTER?

NO WAY, NO HOW. IT'S NOT HAPPENING!
RIGHT.
SIGH
EDITOR MS. N
WHAT, DOES A SECOND-RATE COMIC ARTIST LIKE YOU NEED SOMEONE TO SPELL IT OUT IN CRAYON FOR YOU?
THWOMP
ガーン!
PTOO
I RESENT THAT!
THAT'S TOMINO OVER THERE...
GLUG
SO IT'S IM-POSSIBLE, HUH?
LET'S SEE WHAT THE MAN HIMSELF HAS TO SAY ABOUT IT!
HIDEKI, TAKING OFF!
Wooogh...
GOOD IDEA, THAT WAY WE CAN PUT THIS TO REST, AND–
WHAT ?!

SOMEBODY STOP THAT PSYCHO!
HE'S OUT OF CONTROL!
FWOOM
UM! EXCUSE ME, MR. T-T-TOMINO, SIR!
WHO ARE YOU?
RMMBLL

I WANNA DRAW A MANGA WITH YOU AS THE PRO-TAGONIST, SIR!
GOOONG
THAT IDIOT WENT AND BLURTED IT OUT!
OH GOD.
WE'RE SCREWED!

THE STORY SO FAR... A MANGA ARTIST APPROACHES YOSHIYUKI TOMINO AT A PARTY AND DARES TO REQUEST THE UNTHINKABLE: "I WANNA DRAW A MANGA WITH YOU AS THE PROTAGONIST, SIR!"
RRMMBBLLL
GUNDAM GENESIS
THE UNTOLD STORY
PART 2
RMBL
RMBL
TNK
TNK

WHUD

HE HEAD-BUTTED HIM OUTTA NOWHERE
AT POINT-BLANK RANGE?!
I KNEW IT, HE'S PISSED! ABSOLUTELY ENRAGED!
OH GOD... WE'RE BEYOND SCREWED.
AND IT'S ALL THAT DAMNED MANGA ARTIST'S FAULT!
FSHHH
WOBBL
YANK

DO WHAT YOU WANT!

A SINGLE-LINE FROM THE DIRECTOR. NOTHING MORE.
AND WITH THAT, HE DISAPPEARED BACK INTO THE CROWD.
PLANNING FOR THIS SERIES BEGAN SOON AFTERWARDS.

VISUAL EXAGGERATION ASIDE...

IT'S BASICALLY ALL TRUE.

THE SUMMER OF 1979.
TOMINO LEGENDS
NIPPON SUNRISE
DIRECTOR, ARE YOU THERE?
WHAT'S UP? LOOKIN' FOR A BUTT MASSAGE?
SHWF
SHWF
OW. ANYWAY. WHAT'D YOU WANT?
THRB
THRB
RIGHT!
YOU'VE GOT A PHONE CALL. A MR. NISHIZAWA FROM OFFICE ACADEMY.
RRMBL

THAT OLD SON OF A BITCH...
PART 1
TOMINO LEGENDS
Summer 1979

キャッ
CLK
YEAH?
ザザ
FSSSSHHHH
IT'S BEEN TOO LONG, TOMINO.
YOSHINOBU NISHIZAKI
A BRILLIANT PRODUCER WITH MORE THAN A FEW LEGENDS TO HIS NAME.
YAMATO HAD ACHIEVED MEGA-HIT STATUS A FEW YEARS EARLIER, AND THE WORLD WAS NOW HIS OYSTER.
HONESTLY, I'M SURPRISED YOU'RE STILL IN THE ANIME BIZ.
ザアアアア
FSSSHHHHH
I'VE HEARD RUMORS ABOUT YOU, TOO.
THEY, UH...
THEY AIN'T GREAT.
HEH. *SPARE ME.*

I WANTED TO LET YOU KNOW ABOUT SOMETHING.

トク GLG

トク GLG

YEAH? WHAT?

I'M MAKING TRITON OF THE SEA *INTO A MOVIE.*

INTO A WHAT–?

WITH NISHIZAKI AS PRODUCER, *TRITON OF THE SEA* WAS YOSHIYUKI TOMINO'S DIRECTORIAL DEBUT.

IT HAD SINCE BEEN REDISCOVERED AND HAILED AS A FORGOTTEN CLASSIC.

I GET IT. SO THAT'S WHY YOU CALLED.
SORRY, BUT I'M NOT INTERESTED IN WORKING WITH–
クイ SHWIP
DON'T MISTAKE MY INTEN-TIONS.
YOUR NAME WON'T BE GRACING THE BILLBOARDS.
THE HELL?

AUDIENCES WON'T LINE UP FOR DIRECTOR YOSHIYUKI TOMINO.

...
DON'T SCREW WITH ME, OLD MAN.
TRITON ATE A CANCELLATION, SURE.
BUT I'VE COME A LONG WAY SINCE THEN.

FSSSSHHH

WHATEVER SUCCESS YOU HAVE HAS BEEN WITH TOY COMMERCIALS. I'M MAKING A MOVIE.

I WANT SOMEONE WITH CREDENTIALS DIRECTING. WHAT USE COULD I HAVE FOR YOU?

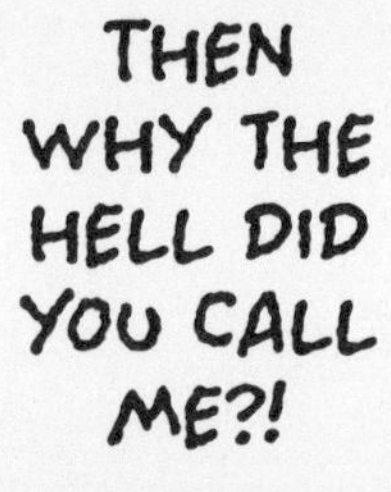

THEN WHY THE HELL DID YOU CALL ME?!

A WORK YOU WERE ONCE INVOLVED WITH WILL SOON BE A FILM.
I THOUGHT IT MIGHT DELIGHT YOU TO KNOW.
DO LOOK FORWARD TO ITS RUN. CIAO.
CLK
BEEP
BEEP

SLAM
ガチャ

WHOOAH
ざわ

THAT SUMMER...

カナ
KREE
カナ
KREE
カナ
KREE

YAMATO FESTIVAL
SPACE BATTLESHIP YAMATO
ARRIVEDERCI YAMATO
TRITON OF THE SEA
TRIPLE FEATURE!
YAMAKOSHI THEATER
山越劇場

TRITON OF THE SEA DEBUTED AS PART OF THE *YAMATO* FESTIVAL.

DID THE WORDS "DIRECTOR: YOSHIYUKI TOMINO" APPEAR IN THE CREDITS?

PRODUCTION
YOSHIYUKI TOMINO

NOT EXACTLY.

HIS NAME WAS LISTED FOR BUT A MOMENT, UNDER PRODUCTION.

KAW
KAW
KAW
KAW
FSSSHHH

CAN'T SAY I'M A FAN OF THAT GUY.
I'VE HEARD SOME NASTY RUMORS ABOUT HIM, TOO.

HEH. JUST THE KIND OF OPINION I'D EXPECT FROM A CHILD.
HUH?

TWO OF THE THREE MOVIES AT THE *YAMATO* FESTIVAL WERE MERE REVIVALS.

KAW

KAW

KAW

THE LAST ONE, *TRITON*, WAS SEVEN YEARS OLD. NO BUDGET. NO NEW SCENES.

BUT THEY STILL PUT IT IN A THEATER AND MADE OUT LIKE BANDITS.

SHWP

DOES SUNRISE HAVE A PRODUCER CAPABLE OF SOMETHING LIKE THAT?

KAW
KAW

...

YOU CAN'T TURN A CORNER IN HOLLYWOOD WITHOUT RUNNING INTO PRODUCERS CREEPIER THAN HIM.

SHWF

YOU'VE GOTTA WHEEL AND DEAL WITH OIL TYCOONS AND INVESTORS.

THAT'S HOW FILMS ARE MADE.

FWHMP

BOOSH

I'M NO HERMIT. CAN'T MAKE ANIME IF IT DOESN'T PUT FOOD ON THE TABLE.

BUT YOU KNOW WHAT? JAPAN'S ANIME BUSINESS IS FINALLY STARTING TO RAKE IT IN.

WAIT, DID WE WORK ON ANYTHING THAT COULD BECOME A MOVIE?
WE NEED TO MAKE SOMETHING HE WON'T BE ABLE TO SCOFF AT.

WE'RE WORKING ON IT *NOW!*
GUNDAM.

THIS WAS RIGHT AS *GUNDAM* WAS ABOUT TO GET CANCELLED FOR LOW RATINGS.

YOU'RE LAUGHING ?!
AHAHA! GUNDAM, HUH?

EEP!
SOUNDS LIKE YOU'RE ASKIN' FOR AN ASS-GRABBIN'!
WHO COULD HAVE IMAGINED IT WOULD BECOME A HIT TWO YEARS LATER?

TOMINO LEGENDS

HAYAKAWA SHOBO'S *S-F MAGAZINE*. THE ELDER STATESMAN OF JAPANESE SCI-FI.

S-F MAGAZINE

COUNTLESS WRITERS STARTED THEIR CAREERS HERE.

AND COUNTLESS MORE STOOD HERE, HOPEFUL, MANUSCRIPTS IN HAND.

S-F MAGAZINE EDITORIAL

THAT SAID.

RRMMMBL

THE PERSON VISITING TODAY IS A LITTLE DIFFERENT FROM THE NORM.

SORRY, I'M NOT SURE I CAUGHT THAT.
LIKE I SAID.
WHAT ARE YOU PROPOS-ING?
FWSH
S-F MAGAZINE E.I.C.
OKA NAU

I'M COOL WITH YOU GUYS RUNNING THE NOVEL VERSION.
PART 2
TOMINO LEGENDS
Winter 1978
スハー
FSHAAAH
...
APOLOGIES, BUT DID YOU PREVIOUSLY ANNOUNCE THE WORK IN QUESTION?
HUH? HELL NO I DIDN'T!
SHKK
THE ANIME'S STARTING SOON, SO
I FIGURED WE COULD RUN THE NOVEL SIDE BY SIDE.

FLP
MOBILE SUIT GUNDAM?

BAM

ABSOLUTELY NOT.

THIS WILL NEVER GRACE THE PAGES OF S-F MAGAZINE.

EXCUSE ME?!

PFT...
A GIANT ROBOT STORY? AND BIPEDAL ONES, AT THAT?
機動戦士ガンダム
GUNDAM
I MEAN, WHAT ARE WE, A TOY MAGAZINE? *HAHAHA!*
HAHAHA!
WE DON'T DEAL IN SUCH PREPOSTEROUS PAP!
SHF
SF
NOW PLEASE LEAVE.
IN THE MODERN DAY, BIPEDAL ROBOTS LIKE ASIMO MAY BE A FACT OF REALITY. IN 1978, THEY WERE A TOY STORE FANTASY.
ASIMO
HONDA
AS FAR AS ANYONE WAS CONCERNED, GUNDAM WAS A TOY COMMERCIAL.
KLNK

SLAM
S-F MAGAZINE'S REACTION WAS A NATURAL ONE.
BUT AS YOU ALL KNOW, *GUNDAM* WENT ON TO BECOME AN EARTH-SHATTERING HIT.

THE *GUNDAM* NOVELS, PUBLISHED BY ASAHI SONORAMA, MOVED A MILLION COPIES.

AN UNTHINKABLE SUCCESS BY SCI-FI STANDARDS.

THERE WAS MUCH GNASHING OF TEETH AT HAYAKAWA SHOBO.

AND THE NOVELS THEMSELVES SENT UNEXPECTED RIPPLES ACROSS TIME AND SPACE.
BOOKS
TSUKISHIMA BOOKS
ざわ
MRR
ざわ
MURR
DOOT-DOO-DOO... ♪

ON SALE TODAY
I WANNA READ SOMETHING COOL...
SUPER EXPRESS109
HM?

MOBILE SUIT GUNDAM?
WEREN'T KIDS IN CLASS GOING NUTS OVER MODEL KITS FOR THAT THING?

I'VE NEVER SEEN IT. WONDER WHAT IT'S ABOUT.
FLP
SOME KINDA ROBOT MANGA?
HRK!
SHDDR
WHOA...

SHBOOM
th towel
apped
ound h
torso..
BLAM
delicate
utline of
er nipples
women
warm,
skin..
BAM
THIS IS GUNDAM ?!
THIS IS WHAT THOSE GUYS HAVE BEEN READING?!
THE NOVELIZATION WAS COMPLETELY DIFFERENT FROM THE ANIME, AND ITS ADULT THEMES DROVE YOUNG MEN ACROSS THE COUNTRY WILD!
BLONDIE!
O-OW!
SHWING

NOW THIS...

YOWWW!

THD

THIS IS LITERATURE!

THE *MOBILE SUIT GUNDAM* NOVELS AWAKENED ALL SORTS OF FEELINGS IN ALL SORTS OF YOUNG MEN.
AND THIS BOY RIGHT HERE WAS ONE OF THEM.

YOU MAY KNOW HIM TODAY— AS FAMOUS WORDSMITH HARUTOSHI FUKUI.

TOMINO LEGENDS
FALL, 1979, AT A STUDIO IN TOKYO.
KA-KLAK
Captain, please wear your normal suit when launching today.
Hrm... If that's what you want, Lalah.
OKAY, PERFECT! BREAKTIME, FOLKS!
CHAR AZNABLE'S VOICE ACTOR SHUICHI IKEDA
MAN, I'M BEAT!
HA HA ♡
...
HM? SOMETHING WRONG, SHU?
BEING AROUND THE SAME AGE, IKEDA AND HIROTAKA SUZUOKI WERE BEST BUDS.
YOU COULD SAY THAT.

THAT LINE JUST NOW MADE ZERO SENSE.
THE ONE ABOUT CHAR LAUNCHING IN HIS NORMAL SUIT?
YEAH. THEY KISS, AND THAT'S WHAT SHE SAYS TO HIM?

PLUS, CHAR'S NOT EVEN WEARING HIS NORMAL SUIT IN THE NEXT SCENE.
BUT LALAH DOESN'T EVEN MENTION IT.
SHIT MAKES NO SENSE!
HOW AM I SUPPOSED TO READ THE LINE?

BWAAAH

PROBABLY JUST AN ANIMATION MIXUP, RIGHT?

I MEAN, HEY, YASUHIKO COLLAPSED. WORD IS THE STUDIO'S A TOTAL MADHOUSE.

PROBABLY HAPPENS ALL THE TIME IN ANIME.

SURE. BUT NOT THIS GUY.

NOT THE DIRECTOR OF *GUNDAM*.

THIS IS YOSHIYUKI TOMINO WE'RE TALKIN' ABOUT.

PART 3

TOMINO LEGENDS

Autumn 1979

YOU'RE RIGHT...

NO WAY IT'S A MISTAKE.

SHF

GOTTA BE A REASON.

FLP

FROM A CONVENTIONAL ANGLE, IT'S WEIRD AS HELL.

FROM A CONVENTIONAL ANGLE...

AH-HA. SO THAT'S HOW IT IS!

HE THOUGHT OF EVERY-THING!
THAT DIRTY OLD DOG!
DIRTY? WHAT ARE YOU TALKING ABOUT, SHU?

FWOOSH
SHU ?!
DIRECTOR, CAN YOU CONFIRM SOMETHING FOR ME?
BAM
WHAT IS IT?

CHAR AND LALAH.

CAN I THINK OF THEM AS... *HOOKED UP?*

HOOKED UP? THIS IS A CARTOON FOR KIDS!
SORRY ABOUT THIS, DIRECTOR! HE'S JUST TIRED, SO—

Heh

BY ALL MEANS.

WAIT, SERIOUSLY?
I KNEW IT.
IT'S NO DIFFERENT THAN IF A GIRLFRIEND TOLD HER MAN NOT TO FORGET HIS UMBRELLA ON A RAINY DAY.

THE GUY SAYS "UH-HUH," BUT CAN'T BE BOTHERED TO ACTUALLY TAKE THE UMBRELLA.
THE WOMAN ISN'T ABOUT TO GET ON HIS CASE FOR IT.

THEY'RE TOO CLOSE FOR THAT.

FROM A CONVENTIONAL ANGLE, CHAR'S JUST A MAN IN AN INTIMATE RELATIONSHIP.
AIN'T THAT RIGHT?

SO THAT'S WHY HE'S NOT WEARING HIS NORMAL SUIT.
HEH. SHUICHI IKEDA. I SHOULD HAVE KNOWN YOU'D BE THE ONLY ONE TO NOTICE.
WHILE WE'RE ON THE SUBJECT...

IN MY HEAD,

I'VE GOT EVEN STEAMIER SCENES IN MIND.

NOW THERE'S SOMETHING I WOULD'VE LIKED TO SEE.

"I REMEMBER ASKING TOMINO—LALAH AND CHAR ARE AN ITEM, RIGHT? IS IT OKAY FOR ME TO PUT THAT INTO MY PERFORMANCE?

SHUICHI IKEDA, FROM *A REQUIEM TO CHA*

BEING A GENIUS, YOSHIKAZU YASUHIKO REALIZED THIS, OF COURSE. HE REDREW MOST OF THE SCENES INVOLVING LALAH AND CHAR FOR THE MOVIE.

BWABAAAAAM
THE END RESULT WAS CONSIDER-ABLY SPICIER.

IT HAD A PROFOUND EFFECT ON SOME PARTICULARLY SENSITIVE MEMBERS OF THE AUDIENCE.

THIS FEELING... CAN IT BE?
DID CHAR AND LALAH DO WHAT I THINK THEY DID?

SHWING
OW!
OW OW!

THMP
OWIE OW OW!
YOU OKAY, MAN?
HARU-TOSHI?!

WHO IS THIS YOUNG MAN, YOU ASK?

NONE OTHER THAN FAMED WRITER HARUTOSHI FUKUI.

OWIE OWIE OW!

TOMINO LEGENDS
NIPPON SUNRISE
SKREEE
SKREEE
GO ON NOW, JUST FORGET ABOUT EVERYTHING...
BATTLE-SCARRED, I'M THE LAST ONE STANDING
I JUST LOVE THIS NEW INSERT SONG, "HERE COMES CHAR"!
"SHINING LALAH" IS GREAT, TOO.
ESPECIALLY THE LYRICS.
THE RECORD *HERE COMES CHAR* WAS RELEASED DURING *GUNDAM*'S ORIGINAL BROADCAST TO RAVE REVIEWS.
シャアが来る
BUT WHO PENNED THE LYRICS?

TOMINO LEGENDS

PART 4

11/21/1979

WHY DID YOU ACCEPT THE JOB OF WRITING THE LYRICS?
WE'RE REALLY BUSY RIGHT NOW.
...
YOU REALLY DON'T KNOW SHIT, HUH?

WHERE DO YOU THINK THEY WRITE THE LYRICS FOR ANIME SONGS?
WHERE? WELL, UH-

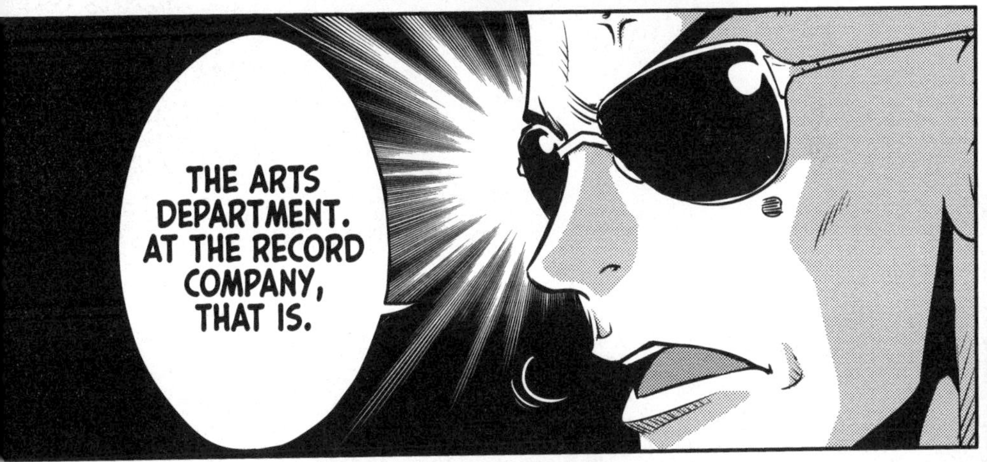

THE ARTS DEPARTMENT. AT THE RECORD COMPANY, THAT IS.

THE ARTS DEPART-MENT?
DON'T THEY DO FAIRY TALES AND NURSERY RHYMES?
YEP. THAT'S RIGHT.
NURSERY
BUZZ BUZZ BUZZ
MOMOTARO

ANIME'S "FOR KIDS," SO IT GETS KIDS' SONGS? BAH.

POP TUNES! NEW MUSIC! ALL OF IT SHOULD BE ON THE TABLE.

BUT ANIME'S BEING HELD BACK. IT'S IN SHACKLES.

Note: New Music was an evolution of Japanese folk music that emerged in the early '70s.

I WROTE THOSE LYRICS TO SHATTER THOSE SHACKLES.
HUH. R-REALLY?

YU AKU'S A FRIEND OF MINE. HE GAVE ME SOME TIPS.
HUH?! YU AKU?
YOU MEAN *THAT* YU AKU ?!

YU AKU.
TSUGARU KAIKYO FUYUGESHIKI. NAGISA NO SINDBAD. FUNA UTA. ANO KANE WO NARASU NO WA ANATA.
HE WAS THE LYRICAL MASTER BEHIND THESE AND MANY OTHER MEGAHITS!

YOU NEED ALL SORTS OF TOOLS TO COME UP WITH LYRICS, TOMINO.
GOTTA REALLY ABSORB FOUR-LINE POETRY AND RHYTHM TO—
YU AKU
Intro to Lyric Writing
How to Write Hit Songs Like Yu Aku
by Yu Aku
YOU'RE JUST REPEATING STUFF FROM YOUR BOOK!
THAT'S NOT WHAT I WANNA KNOW ABOUT!
TELL ME THE TRICK TO WRITING SONGS THAT'LL GRAB FOLKS BY THE HEART AND NEVER LET GO!
GRRR
RRMMBL
THAT'S WHEN HE TOLD ME.

THERE'S NO TRICK, DAMMIT!
HE LIVED UP TO THE LEGEND.
HIS WORDS WERE SUCCINCT AND TO THE POINT.
...
BUT I'M NOT GIVING UP!
SHF
GRRK
I WILL WRITE A CHART-TOPPING HIT!

HEE HEE... RIN IOGI'S A PRETTY COOL PEN NAME, AT LEAST.
YEAH, IT'S GOT AN ETHEREAL KINDA RING TO IT.
WHERE'D IT COME FROM?
WHAT STATION DOES NIPPON SUNRISE CALL HOME?
HUH? KAMI-IGUSA, ON THE SEIBU LINE. WHY?

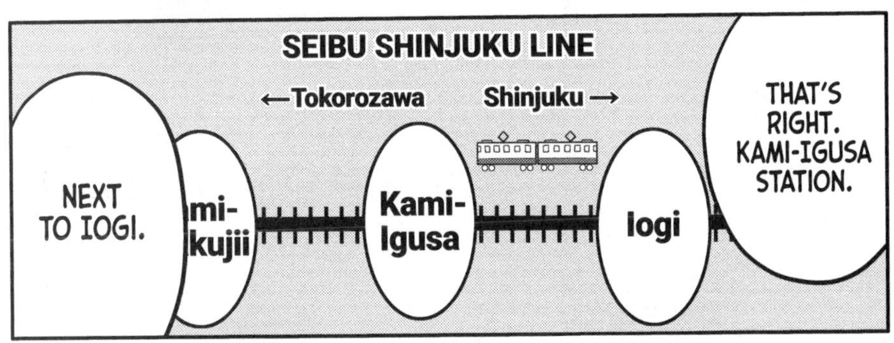

SUNRISE IS NEXT TO IOGI. ERGO...

(BORDE-) RIN' IOGI.

OH MY GOD...

IT WAS A PUN?!

Note: *Soldiers of Sorrow* is on the left, with *Encounter* on the right.

TRUE TO HIS WORD, RIN IOGI WOULD GO ON TO CREATE HIT SONGS.
SOLDIERS OF SORROW AND ENCOUNTER WERE BOTH FEATURED ON THE BEST TEN MUSIC SHOW.
機動戦士ガンダム II
哀戦士
風にひとりで
井上大輔
ガンダムIII
めぐりあい
MOBILE SUIT GUNDAM

AND PEOPLE ARE STILL SINGING THEM NOW, IN THE 21ST CENTURY.

MARCH, 1981
TOKYO. TOKYO.
SHRREEEEE
TOMINO LEGENDS
IKEDA! DIRECTOR TOMINO! I BOUGHT SOME TE—
YOW, THAT'S HOT!
BLUB
HRK!

RMMMBL
TOMINO LEGENDS
PART 5
3/14/1981

YOU'VE REALLY GOTTA DROP THE DEATH STARES.

WHY DO YOU THINK WE'RE GOING TO OSAKA?

TO PREMIERE THE FILM VERSION OF *MOBILE SUIT GUNDAM!*

YEAH

WE'RE IN THE MOVIE BIZ NOW!

DAMN RIGHT WE ARE.

YOU AGREE THIS IS MOVIE BUSINESS, AIN'T IT?

Y-YEAH?

GRRR

THEN WHY'RE ME AND THE DIRECTOR HERE?

THEY STUCK OUR ASSES IN SECOND-CLASS SEATS!

SECOND-CLASS? THAT'S SO OLD-FASHIONED!
THEY'RE CALLED NON-RESERVED SEATS NOW!
AND I'M THE STAR, SO...
SAME FREAKIN' DIFFERENCE!

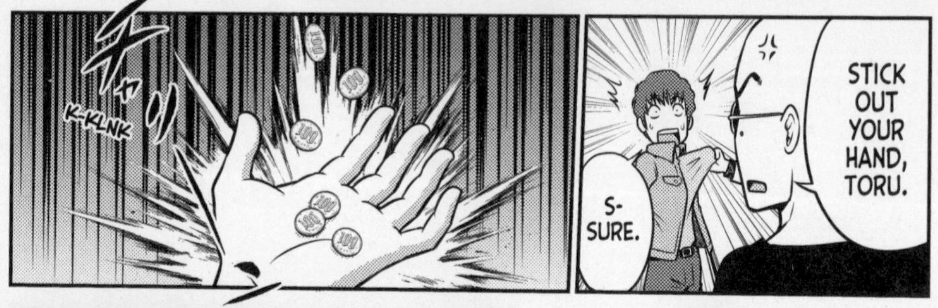

STICK OUT YOUR HAND, TORU.
S-SURE.
K-KLNK

LISTEN UP. THIS BULLET TRAIN'S GOT A PUBLIC PHONE.

SHFF

USE IT TO CALL THE PRESIDENT OF SHOCHIKU. ASK HIM ONE SIMPLE QUESTION.

WHEN THEY PREMIERE THE *TORA-SAN* MOVIES...

DOES THAT CREW GO SECOND-FREAKIN'-CLASS?!

ER, KIYOSHI ATSUMI AND DIRECTOR YAMADA PROBABLY GET FIRST-CLASS SEATS, RIGHT?
JUST MAKE THE DAMN PHONE CALL!
SIR!
SHHHPP

WAAAUGH!

FHWOOOM

BACK IN 1981, SHOCHIKU DIDN'T THINK MUCH OF ANIME FILMS.

THAT CHANGED WHEN *GUNDAM* AND *GUNDAM II: SOLDIERS OF SORROW* BECAME HITS.

哀戦士

風にひとりで

井上大輔

機動戦士ガンダム

WHEN *GUNDAM III* OPENED IN THEATERS THE FOLLOWING YEAR, IT WAS A FULL-BLOWN PHENOMENON.

SUIT GUNDAM

THE COMPANY HAD TO ACKNOWLEDGE IT.
...
AH, FIRST-CLASS REALLY IS SOMETHIN' ELSE!
MY ASS IS LOVIN' THIS SEAT!
KTNK
KTNK
MM-HM.
GREEN CAR

AND THEN TORU TAKES A DIFFERENT JOB WITHOUT EVEN REALIZING SHOCHIKU FRONTED THE CASH FOR US TO RIDE PREMIUM! TALK ABOUT MISSING OUT!
HAHAHA! TOTALLY.

HM?
TORU AND HANNY?
OH, HELLO, CAPTAIN.
AHH!

HA HA HA

LALAH AND AMURO GONNA BE JOINING US AT THE PREMIERE?

I'M AFRAID NOT.

HUH?

WE'RE HELPING WITH THE PREMIERE OF TOEI'S *QUEEN MILLENNIA*.

FURUYA PLAYS A MAJOR CHARACTER TOO. DAISUKE YAMORI, YES?

Y-YUP!

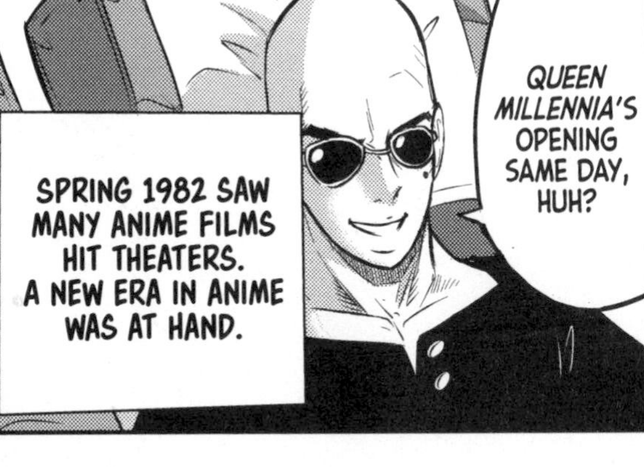

BKRRK

YOU'RE OUR PROTAGONIST! THE HELL ARE YOU DOING AT THEIR PREMIERE?!

RRRGHHH

S-SIR, THERE'S A REASON, I CAN EXPLAIN!
Y'SEE...
TOEI OFFERED WAY BETTER CASH AND TREATMENT THAN SHOCHIKU, SO—

YOU'RE DEAD, TORU!
SHWOOOM
WAAAAUGH! FORGIVE ME, SIR!

A *GUNDAM* COMPUTER GAME?

THAT RIGHT?

PART 6

TOMINO LEGENDS

December 1983

COMPUTERS AREN'T EXACTLY IN EVERY HOUSEHOLD, ARE THEY?

YOU'RE RIGHT. COMPUTERS WERE ONCE MASSIVE MACHINES. HARDLY HOUSEHOLD ELECTRONICS.

BUT PERSONAL COMPUTERS ARE STARTING TO BECOME MORE COMMON.

WHY, THE GUNDAM WAS INSTALLED WITH A LEARNING COMPUTER ITSELF. A PERSONAL COMPUTER, IF YOU WILL.

AND AS LUCK WOULD HAVE IT,

IT IS NOW POSSIBLE FOR US

TO SET OFF FOR ADVENTURE IN SIDE-7 AS AMURO RAY HIMSELF!

SHOW ME.
I'LL GET IT READY.
NYAA
にやり
BAAAM
FM-7 MAZE

THE UNIVERSAL CENTURY IS CLOSE AT HAND.
FWK
KCHACK
SCRRRCH
ZHHHK
BEEEP
SCRRCH
BEEEP
SCRRRRCH
BEEP
BEEP

IT'S STILL NOT READY?
HOLD ON JUST A LITTLE LONGER!

AH, SOME-THING'S THERE!

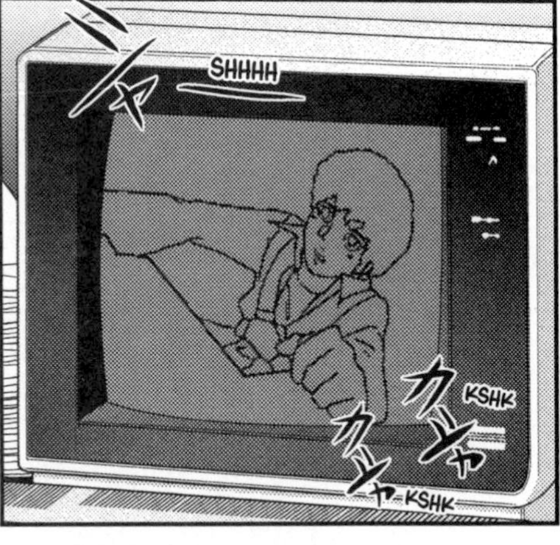
SHHHH
KSHK
KSHK

BEEEP

DON'T TELL ME. YOU HAVE TO WAIT A FEW MINUTES EVERY TIME THE SCREEN CHANGES?
SEEMS LIKE IT.

機動戦士
ガンダム
GUNDAM
Real-time
Role-playing
Adventure game.
Part 1
GUNDAM STANDS!
ADVENTURE GAMES AT THE TIME HAD TO DRAW THEIR GRAPHICS ON THE SCREEN LINE BY LINE. NEEDLESS TO SAY, IT WAS TIME CONSUMING.

HOOT
HOOT
NIPPON SUNRISE
WHEW...
11. You see Elecar and ZAK far away.
est. There is ZAK near by.
NOW A ZAKU'S ATTACKING, HUH?

KCHAK
SCREW IT!
Command:? HIT ZAK
OH DEAR, YOU SHOULDN'T-

BEEEP
GAME OVER
HM?
LET ME GUESS. BACK TO THE BEGINNING?

IS... IS THIS GAME SELLING?
NO SHIT, HUH. COLOR ME IMPRESSED.
HUH? OH, WELL. HERE AND THERE.
HAHA! IT'S HARDLY ANYTHING SPEC—

I'M NOT TALKING ABOUT WHOEVER MADE THIS THING.

I'M TALKING ABOUT THE PSYCHOS PLAYING IT.

IT'S BEEN MORE THAN A DECADE SINCE THE START OF THE 21ST CENTURY,

BUT THERE'S STILL NO GAME THAT LETS YOU EXPLORE SIDE-7 AS AMURO.

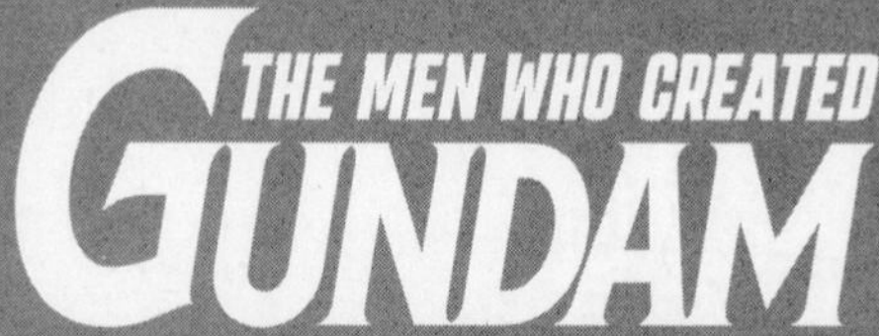
THE MEN WHO CREATED
GUNDAM

TOMINO LEGENDS
DIVAS!
THE GLAMOROUS FLOWERS THAT DEFINE GENERATIONS!
HIBARI MISORA, MOMOE YAMAGUCHI, SEIKO MATSUDA...
THESE ARE BUT A FEW OF THE NAMES THAT COME TO MIND.
SHNG
BUT A CERTAIN SEGMENT OF HARDCORE GUNDAMENTALISTS WILL ADAMANTLY INSIST OTHERWISE.
THERE CAN ONLY BE ONE TRUE DIVA.

To the slumbering blue~♪

AND HER NAME IS PIROKO MORIGUCHI!

TOMINO LEGENDS

PART 7

8/5/1985

ANNOUNCING
Zeta Gundam's
NEW OPENING SONG
RMMMBL
RAHH
RAHH
RAHH
WOW, SHE'S ADORABLE! THAT'S A REAL IDOL FOR YOU!
—SUMMER 1985

JIGGL

NEW
A BIG ROUND OF APPLAUSE FOR PIROKO MORIGUCHI! NOW THEN, LET'S HAVE DIRECTOR TOMINO COME ON STAGE!
DIRECTOR TOMINO!
BOW
UM, DIRECTOR?
DON'T TELL ME...
HUH?
SHE'S GOT A NICE ASS.

DON'T MIND IF I DO!
TNGL
TNGL
HE'S RARING TO GO!
HOOEEEYO♥
NO! WE'RE SECONDS AWAY FROM A SEXUAL HARASSMENT CHARGE!
ドドドドド
VOOMM
SHE'S AN IDOL WITH AN AGENCY! IF THAT HAND MAKES CONTACT, WE'RE DONE FOR!
DIRECTOR TOMINO!! STO-OOO-OOP!!

GRRRMP
JOLT
WHADDAYA THINK YOU'RE DOING?
KRRK
KRRK

MY ASS DOESN'T COME CHEAP, Y'KNOW.
ROOAR
LET'S HEAR ONE MORE SONG! SILVER DRESS!
Zeta Gundam
NEW OPENING SONG
DIREC-TOR?
HELL OF A WOMAN. NOT A DIME-A-DOZEN IDOL, THAT'S FOR SURE.
HUH?

ALL THE MORE REASON I GOTTA TOUCH THAT ASS.

UNFORTUNATELY, PIROKO MORIGUCHI STRUGGLED TO RECORD A HIT IN THE YEARS TO COME.

THE AGENCY ADVISED HER TO RECONSIDER HER IDOL CAREER.

BUT PIROKO REMAINED UNDAUNTED.

"I'LL DO WHATEVER IT TAKES," SHE ANNOUNCED. AND WHATEVER IT TAKES, SHE DID. VARIETY SHOWS. SKETCH COMEDY. IMPRESSIONS. SHE THREW HERSELF HEADLONG INTO WORK NO IDOL HAD DONE BEFORE.

EVENTUALLY, HER EFFORTS WERE RECOGNIZED. LIKE A PHOENIX, SHE WAS REBORN!

AND IN SO DOING, SHE FORGED NEW GROUND AS THE WORLD'S FIRST VARIETY IDOL!

RRRMMMBBLL

ゴゴゴゴ

IN 1991, TOMINO HAD HIS FATEFUL SECOND ENCOUNTER WITH PIROKO MORIGUCHI.

BUT SHE WAS NO LONGER AN IDOL. SHE WAS A SONGSTRESS, ESTEEMED IN HER OWN RIGHT.

RAAAH
LIKE I TOLD YOU.
MY BUTT DOESN'T COME CHEAP.

AS TO WHETHER YOSHIYUKI TOMINO EVER SUCCESSFULLY GRABBED THAT ASS...

NO RECORD EXISTS TO DOCUMENT IT.

THE MEN WHO CREATED
GUNDAM

Guest Columns

These columns are to be read left to right. Since they are not single page long or two-page spreads like the previous essays, we wanted to inform our readers of where these columns start to avoid confusion.

Masanobu Komaki's starts on page 543 and runs through page 541.

Makoto Togashi's starts on page 547 and continues through page 544.

I saw no reason to object. They represent *Gundam* fans across Japan, standing in for the nameless many who ardently supported *Mobile Suit Gundam* during its bleakest moments of abject unpopularity, eventually becoming fans whose passion etched *Gundam* into the history books.

The small and unassuming male fan is an unvarnished representation of middle and high schoolers with long commutes, who raced home every day after club activities ended. There was no easy access to information at the time, and video tape players, while readily available, still cost around $3,000.

The female fan represents those who lived outside Tokyo and the major cities. With no one in their class to talk about anime with, they would travel all the way to cafes in the big city to find someone conversant in the language of *Gundam*.

Though they are composite characters, their actions and words are true to the lived experience of actual fans from the time period.

It's been more than 35 years since the events depicted in this story, and the world has changed immensely. Fans at the time communicated through postcards and letters. There were no cell phones. Nonetheless, the time it takes to travel from Sunrise's office in Kami-Igusa to ALTA by way of Seibu Shinjuku Station hasn't changed a bit.

Anime broadcasts transitioned to digital, their screen ratios upgraded to 16:9. The traditional production flow of capturing painted cels on film no longer exists, but just like 35 years ago, the quality of an animator's key frames still decides everything.

For readers under the age of 35 born after the One Year War, I hope the story depicted in the pages of this book resonates with that same feeling of the new we experienced back then. That said, I also have to emphasize the degree to which it's playing with fire. Here's hoping nobody gets upset over the way they were depicted! ◆

Masanobu Komaki

Former editor-in-chief of *Animec*. After *Animec* ceased publication, he became E.I.C. of Rapport Publishing, where he handled planning and editing duties on mooks and manga. He also serves as a sci-fi setting supervisor for various media. In November 2003, he founded Studio Komaki, using his considerable connections and extensive know-how to explore new means of expression. He's also a lecturer at Josai International University's anime and manga media studies program.

anecdotes, it is *not* my fault the character turned out the way she did. (Just covering my bases—all five of them are still working in the industry.)

I was also asked for details about what it was like in *Animec*'s editorial department at the time. All told, the first discussion we had took roughly two hours. Imagine my surprise, then, when I was suddenly informed I would be appearing as a character in the next issue! Mr. N sent me the storyboards, and I was even *more* surprised. Shocked, really. *This isn't accurate,* I thought.

"Just so you know, *Animec* didn't have the money for a video cassette player back then."

"It's fine. This *is* a gag manga, after all."

As a manga editor myself, there is no greater suffering than dealing with unreasonable requests from clients during submissions. As far as I'm concerned, a gag manga author should be able to get away with anything so long as it makes the reader laugh. In reality, however, clients always want things changed. Hence my decision to throw my hands up in the air and let Ohwada do whatever he felt like when depicting the fictional Masanobu Komaki in the story.

In the actual *Animec* screening room, for example, we removed the phone lines and locked the door to ensure nobody interrupted. That's how we watched *Mobile Suit Gundam*. When I saw the way my first viewing of *Gundam* was depicted in the manga, I figured, hey, why sweat the details? I did make one request, however.

"I wasn't into *Lulu, the Flower Angel* back then, but *Anne of Green Gables*."

"Gotcha. I'll adjust things accordingly."

Needless to say, Mr. N is not to be trifled with. After that, they'd send me the roughs for checking, and I'd limit my suggestions to clarifying details as the series continued. When someone would complain about the way someone was depicted, I'd intervene, saying, "It's a gag manga. Who's going to take this seriously?" And to think, I was just an outside consultant...

I wonder—is it really okay to write this work off as a mere gag manga? I don't think there's another piece of media that better conveys the enthusiasm of the animators and fans at the time. It really makes you feel the passion from that heady era, perhaps even better than the New Anime Century Declaration documentary NHK aired to celebrate *Gundam*'s 30th anniversary.

In some ways, it's precisely *because* it's a comedy that it's able to best convey the truth. It gets to sidestep the red tape that would normally prevent certain stories from seeing the light of day, and frankly portray the sentiment of the show's young creators and viewers. After all: *it's just a gag manga.*

The only characters who completely diverge from reality are two fans who appear at the end of the New Anime Century Declaration. Ohwada was adamant that they be composite stand-ins for the actual fans of the time period.

GUEST COLUMN **Masanobu Komaki** (Former E.I.C. of anime magazine *Animec*)

"BOY, THIS IS really something," I thought as I read the first episode of "Gundam Genesis" with detached bemusement. As far as works dedicated to needling Yoshiyuki Tomino go, this surely ranks among the pantheon. I don't believe I've seen anyone else attempt to portray Yasuhiko this way, either. His work is published in the pages of the very same magazine (*Gundam Ace*), yet Mr. Ohwada caricatured him anyway. That surprised me the most, I think.

Even Okawara, a designer renowned for his care and attention to detail, is portrayed as a foreman at an ironworks. As I excitedly flipped through the pages, I couldn't help but wonder, "Is this okay?" Up until this point, it had all been someone else's problem. Then I got a call from a supervisor on the project, one Mr. N, and I realized you should never assume you'll always be a bystander.

Truth be told, there was no other writer back in 1979 who was visiting Sunrise for coverage every week, so when they asked me to offer my recollections of the time, I had plenty of anecdotes to offer.

What Ohwada asked me for help on first was a female point-of-view character. I didn't need to invent anything; a composite of the women I saw working in the planning office was more than sufficient. We'd refer to them as production assistants today, and the job they performed required a very specific skill: the ability to relay opinions to Tomino directly, *without* him flipping his lid.

As such, you can think of Momoe Kusakari as both a fictional character within the manga's story, and a composite of five women who actually worked at Sunrise. That said, while I provided the

But then I think back 35 years. Back to when I was a college student, all bright-eyed and bushy tailed. I was raised in no small part by *Gundam*, but to others, they might describe it differently. They might say that before they realized it, they were being controlled by a Gundam that was inside *them*. Like their energy is being drained away.

Here's what I think. *Gundam* is made of the thoughts and emotions of people, and it lives on in them, too. The emotions of everyone who gathered in front of Shinjuku Station's east exit on that fateful day. The emotions of everyone who diligently made their way to the movie theaters to see it. The emotions of everyone who built Gunpla. *Gundam* lives on in that steadily expanding breadth of lived experience.

Ever since that day in 1981, we've been lucky enough to pour our passion and emotion into this thing we call *Gundam*, watching it grow and change along the way. There is nothing else like it. We are truly blessed.

Thank you for reading my ramblings up until this point. At the very least, I hope it served as a brief glimpse into a particular era of history. ◆

camera and helped with recording. I wore a Zaku suit and volunteered myself to get a Buff Clan haircut. It was craziness on a scale I would never again witness. After graduating, I started working for a publishing and video company. No matter the project, I never found any of the planning or sales work they threw at me particularly painful. I can probably thank my experience working on *Ideon* for that.

Let's return to *Gundam* for a moment. Our circle ran a *Gundam* feature in one of the doujinshi zines we put out, and I actually went up to Tokyo with the president and a few other members during summer vacation to interview Director Tomino himself. I'm not sure if it's because Tomino was wowed by the president's letter, or by the fact that the president was female, but in any case, he came all the way out to a cafe in Shinjuku to chat with us. We were just some college students, but he still chatted at length with us about *2001: A Space Odyssey* and film theory. Thinking about it now, the impact from the work itself, alongside those kinds of personal experiences, naturally led me to pursuing a career in visual media.

Becoming acutely aware of the kind of thought processes involved in creating a work like *Gundam* helped me realize the expressive potential of anime itself. It was also the origin of my interest in video production. Never in my wildest dreams could I imagine that fifteen years after I graduated from university, I would be assigned as project producer for its 20th anniversary. It's probably safe to say the experience I had with *Gundam* beginning in '79 impacted my life considerably.

This brings us to autumn '98. The project celebrating *Gundam*'s 20th anniversary would begin the following year, and the theme I chose for it was "Returning the favor to *Gundam*."

We were able to lead the way in bringing *Gundam* back into the limelight, but we were only able to do it thanks to the efforts of countless individuals. I could sense their shared appreciation for *Gundam* every single day we worked on the project. *Gundam* had enriched every one of our lives. We had to return the favor.

Now let's jump forward another 15 years to *Gundam*'s 35th anniversary in 2014. A life-sized statue of the Gundam stands tall in Odaiba, overlooking Tokyo Bay. Footage from the shows are being projected onto the sides of entire buildings. Who could have ever imagined that we'd one day be able to watch *Gundam* in massive all-view domed theaters? Truly remarkable.

As an aside, I feel truly grateful to have been given the honor to work as the producer for such a project. It was not without significant struggle, of course. Nor was it easy. But to me, *Gundam* is a curious thing. It feels like whatever you pour into it inevitably gives rise to something else.

Gundam truly has an odd, almost mystic quality to it. Watching the TV series Blu-Rays that came out in 2013, I found myself with unexpected feelings about the characters. I was surprised at how prone to violence Amuro was and wondered why people tended to pigeonhole him as a loner.

two choices you had for communication, so being able to find and talk with people who shared similar interests felt unbelievably precious. These were allies who loved the same things I did, after all.

That's why we started doing *Gundam* cosplay, too. It garnered attention at events, sure, but it was also a means of communication. A tool to get people on board and get them interested in reading your doujinshi.

It's hard to remember exactly how things ended up the way they did, but eventually events were requesting us. We'd go up on stage before they kicked things off, and even perform—in a way that was both terrifying to me personally and unthinkable today. *Gundam* was powerful enough to make us do stuff like that. It went beyond *liking* the show. I felt joy when we got a laugh from the event audience. When we got interviewed by *Animage*, they took a group photo of us on the streets of Shinjuku for a special cover page feature—something that I'm both proud of, and slightly embarrassed by. Just one of those things that only could have happened then.

I believe those are the things that led to us being contacted to help promote the film. Honestly, it felt slightly surreal at the time; especially the day of. February 22, 1981, arrived like a hurricane. In the morning, we got called over to the Shochiku Theater in Shinjuku to do... something. Was that the fashion show?

From there, we had a meeting in a cafe, where we were shown the New Anime Century Declaration. They said they wanted a representative to read it aloud. We were compensated for the day with sandwiches at the cafe, which was honestly enough for us. We believed in what Nobe told us, without a doubt in our hearts... "Today's the starting point. We're going to see new talents even younger than you appear, one after the other. The start of a new era in anime."

We trusted in that message completely.

After that, many of our friends and colleagues pursued careers in the anime industry and related fields, creating new works and forms of media. Did the way things develop match the ideal Nobe had in mind? Honestly, I don't know if I can answer that.

The youthful new talents and discoveries we expected certainly arrived, but in many ways, I think a lot of it may have trickled over to the game industry. Did that event in Shinjuku mark the start of an actual *New Anime Century*? I'm honestly not sure.

Speaking personally, *Ideon* ended up being the biggest turning point for me, as I got to work with Nobe on it as an assistant film advertising producer. This was around the time I was a senior in college, with about 3 months until *The IDEON* opened in theaters. I had no idea what I was doing. It was me and a handful of newbie assistants making two TV specials (30 minutes and 90 minutes, respectively) for the *Ideon* promo events Nobe was holding at Harumi, Harajuku, and the like. I helped with everything. Production support, paperwork, creating scripts for the phone workers. I even appeared on

GUEST COLUMN Makoto Togashi (Producer: *Gothicmade*)

—How exactly did *Gundam* influence me at the start of the '80s?

I first met "Uncle" Tadahiko Nobe, the 35-year-old advertising producer for the film version of *Gundam*, during my junior year of university. I was 21, and his words had an unbelievably profound impact on me. He told us, "You may be viewers right now, but going forward, you'll be creators. That's where the future of anime begins."

We met Nobe in January of '81 (I think), when Komaki, the EIC of *Animec*, told fans like us that he wanted our help to get the word out about the movie version of *Mobile Suit Gundam*. I remember him saying something like, "Grown-ups don't get it. If we're going to get them to understand *Gundam*, we need your help." That was all we needed to hear. We decided on the spot to help out. *It's now or never!*

Who were "we"? We were members of an anime and manga fan circle known as Arcadian Kyoto. As you might have guessed from the name, it was headquartered in Kyoto, with more than 70 members nationwide at its peak. Actually, it might have been closer to 100. The average member was in their early 20s, or maybe younger. Why did the powers that be decide to reach out to mere fans like us? Let me think back a bit...

In the circle I was originally part of, we were fans of Leiji Matsumoto, (hence the name *Arcadian*) and shared our appreciation for his work through doujinshi that contained writing, illustrations, and manga. All of the members other than the president were... big fans of festivals? Had a surprising love of sports? Were really sociable? Whatever the case, we loved getting together and doing stuff. Most of the members were college students or folks with full-time jobs, but we had middle and high schoolers in our ranks, too, so we went on trips together, hung out by the river, held picnics... I think we organized volleyball and softball games, too? As clubs like these tended to do, we also rented out booths at doujinshi events.

This was right between the end of the '70s and the start of the '80s, when Comic Market was held at the Ota Industrial Building and the Kawasaki Shimin Plaza. From my recollections, there were a little over 300 circles in attendance, with around 6-7,000 attendees. It wasn't a huge community. As for what we *did* there...

While selling doujinshi was our stated goal, we were mostly there just to meet up and hang out. We'd go around to different booths to check out the wares and buy stuff, and if we heard there was a killer artist in attendance, we'd head over to check out their doujinshi.

To give you an idea of what kind of era this was, we still had black rotary phones in our homes. Email and fax machines didn't exist. The internet and cell phones were still the stuff of sci-fi. Talking and writing letters were effectively the only

THE MEN WHO CREATED
GUNDAM